HARRY A. HILL

FIGHTER!

A GUIDE TO LIFE AND BUSINESS

ADVANCE PRAISE

"Harry's book *Fighter! A Guide to Life and Business* is a compelling and insightful resource recounting his journey to success as a businessman and a person. His invaluable advice and real-life examples make this book essential reading. I have known Harry for more than ten years, and he is a person who has made a mark for himself and made a difference. The fact that he achieved this in a foreign country makes his story all the more inspiring."
Takeshi Niinami, Representative Director, President and CEO, Suntory Holdings Limited

"Harry's book *Fighter! A Guide to Life and Business* is a compelling testament to his unwavering dedication to both business success and the fighting spirit. His valuable insights resonate deeply with our mission at UFC Gym, where we aim to empower individuals to embrace the fighting spirit in all aspects of their lives. His book not only offers practical business advice but also embodies the resilience, determination, and relentless spirit that we strive to instill in our members. It is a valuable resource that aligns perfectly with our mission and will undoubtedly inspire and empower our community to overcome obstacles and achieve greatness, both inside and outside the Octagon."
Adam Sedlak, CEO, UFC Gym

"Harry Hill is one of Japan's great serial entrepreneurs. He tells us a great story and provides valuable lessons in leadership, a leadership approach steeped in purpose and always powered by a plan. Harry shares his experience of giving all of himself with passion and determination, resulting in success not only for himself, but also for all fortunate to be touched by him."
Thiery Porte, Vice Chairman and Managing Director, J.C. Flowers & Co.

"*Fighter! A Guide to Life and Business* is a deeply personal and profound reflection of his resilience and unwavering dedication. Together, we have faced numerous challenges and celebrated many victories, and I have witnessed firsthand his incredible journey. His book offers valuable insights into overcoming obstacles and serves as a testament to the strength of our enduring friendship and mutual support in navigating the highs and lows of our entrepreneurial endeavors."
Robert Roche, Founder, Chairman and CEO, Oak Lawn Marketing

"*Fighter! A Guide to Life and Business* is a powerful reflection of Harry's unwavering commitment and deep understanding of the principles of resilience and success. As a Sumo wrestler who has also found success in Japan, I can truly appreciate the wisdom, experience, obstacles and insights he shares. His journey and guidance not only resonate with me on a personal level, but also serve as an inspiration to those navigating their own paths to success in unfamiliar territories. Good job, brother."
Konishiki, Trailblazing Sumo wrestler and athlete

Published by
LID Publishing
An imprint of LID Business Media Ltd.
LABS House, 15-19 Bloomsbury Way,
London, WC1A 2TH, UK

info@lidpublishing.com
www.lidpublishing.com

A member of:

BPR ⊛
businesspublishersroundtable.com

© Harry A. Hill, 2024
© LID Business Media Limited, 2024

ISBN: 978-1-915951-43-4
ISBN: 978-1-915951-44-1 (ebook)

Cover and page design: Caroline Li

HARRY A. HILL

FIGHTER!

A GUIDE TO LIFE AND BUSINESS

MADRID | MEXICO CITY | LONDON
BUENOS AIRES | BOGOTA | SHANGHAI

CONTENTS

*"Do not wait to strike till this iron is hot;
but make it hot by striking."*
William Butler Yeats

PROLOGUE

"Fighting out of the red corner, the President and CEO of Shop Japan, Harry Hill."

I can hear the announcer's voice saying my name. I am standing in the dark by myself, backstage. A few meters in front of me, on my left, is an archway, an opening. A spotlight shines on it, but I am out of view.

I arrived at the site of my fight a little before 4 pm. My name was announced just after 10.00. Six hours is a long time to wait — a lot of time to reflect, to remember.

The day is 16 November, 2015, a Monday. The venue is the grand ballroom at Happo-en, a beautiful event hall with spacious gardens in the middle of Tokyo. The ring is standard size, surrounded by more than 30 tables. The audience is a diverse mix of corporate leaders, celebrities, entertainment industry figures and politicians. The Prime Minister's wife is in attendance. There are eight fights scheduled, six amateur and two professional. I am an amateur, but my bout is the main event. Tonight, I am the biggest name on the card.

The waiting seems endless until it suddenly stops. There are only two fights left before mine. Suddenly, the world speeds up. There is no longer enough time to get ready. There is not enough time to stretch, hit the mitts, get a bit of final advice on strategy.

I jerk back to the present.

The first chords of U2's song, *Elevation*, start to play. I wait. This is my moment. I choose the time to enter. I wait for the world to slow down, to beat to my rhythm.

Ten seconds. Twenty seconds. Bono's voice is singing, "Ooh, ooh, ooh." I start to bounce up and down to the rhythm. I was never a great dancer, but somehow, when I kickbox, I can find the rhythm. I can let myself go.

"High, higher than the sun,
You shoot me from a gun,
I need you to elevate me here ..."

I start shuffling forward. I enter the doorway; the spotlight is on me. I am vaguely aware as the crowd applauds my entrance. I start down the walkway to the ring. As I go a few steps forward, my second, Danilo Zanolini, a former kickboxing World Champion, falls in line behind me.

I make my way to the ring. I climb in. My opponent is slightly shorter. At the weigh-in yesterday, he registered about one kilogram heavier. He is stocky, powerful-looking, and about 13 years younger.

The ring clears. It is just the two of us and the referee. The bell rings. He fights orthodox. I fight southpaw. He throws a vicious low kick to my front leg. I had seen video footage of his fighting style. He is better than the video. Much better.

He throws another hard low kick, followed by a jab and a straight. I defend. He throws another combination. I still focus on defense. I haven't countered or engaged. I continue this way for the first 30 seconds.

I can hear concern in Danilo's voice. "What are you doing? Fight." At the ringside I can see the event's organizer, Akemi Nitta, another famous fighter, start to fidget.

The world continues to slow down. This was my plan. I am the matador, the master. I control the ring. I stop the next low kick with my knee and deliver a straight punch, followed by a middle kick. We trade punches for the rest of the round, and I feel my opponent losing confidence and momentum.

In round two I take control. Halfway through, I fake a middle kick and rock my opponent with a straight left. He doesn't go down, but he doesn't entirely recover.

Midway through the round, a group in the audience starts chanting. "Shacho, Shacho ..." which means CEO. I have dictated the fight. This is my time. This is my story.

The bell rings. My opponent and I hug in the middle of the ring. Enemies no longer, we stand on either side of the referee. "And the winner ... Harry Hill!"

I am on the top of the world. "Shop Japan CEO Enters the Ring," is one of the top headlines on *Yahoo! News. GQ* does a story. Two months later, I'm one of six CEOs featured on the New Year's Special of one of the highest-rated Sunday news programs.

In less than two years, however, I will be brought to my knees. Worn down, I resign as President and CEO of Oak Lawn Marketing, Shop Japan. I have to start again.

I am not a professional fighter, but I am a fighter. For me, fighting is more than a way to survive. Fighting is about finding a purpose. I don't fight people as much as I fight for something. Sometimes, I fight alone, but I have been at my best and strongest when I have led people to fight with me, for a clear and meaningful purpose.

I have had highs and lows. I know what it's like to win and I know what it's like to crawl on the canvas. But I keep fighting.

INTRODUCTION

WHO AM I?

I was born in California in 1963, but grew up in the New York area. I came to Japan for the first time in 1985, as a 22-year-old. After three years and getting married, I returned to New York for a year in 1989 to work on Wall Street. I returned to Japan in January of 1990 and, finding myself unemployable, started my first business there.

I became a serial entrepreneur. I have run businesses small and large, with employees numbering from one to five, 10, 50, 100 and more than 500. I have led the negotiations to sell some of these businesses, with valuations ranging from tens of thousands of dollars to almost $700 million.

The major company I led, Oak Lawn Marketing (OLM), which does business as Shop Japan, punches above its weight. In my last full fiscal year as CEO, we recorded our highest-ever sales, at just under ¥70 billion. We had good profitability. In fact, we were the most profitable subsidiary of the NTT Docomo Group, a mobile phone and IT services conglomerate, after it purchased a majority interest in the company in April of 2009.

OLM/Shop Japan (OLM/SJ) is known as a hit maker. Our products are omnipresent in Japan. In 2007, we turned the exercise DVD set *Billy's Bootcamp* into a cultural phenomenon, selling more than 1.5 million units and generating ¥19.5 billion in revenue in just under 11 months. In 2015 and 2016, our Wonder Core exercise device became a viral hit worldwide. With these products, we essentially created the home fitness market in Japan. We also created the mattress overlay market with our best-selling brand, True Sleeper.

While completing this book's first draft, I visited my friend and business partner, Eric Chang. Eric, the founder and president of the health and fitness company Wondercise, designed the Wonder Core concept. Between 2015 and 2017, OLM/SJ sold more than 6 million units of the Wonder Core series of products, with almost $1 billion in sales.

Eric was successful before meeting us, but our partnership propelled him to new heights. Building on the momentum of OLM/SJ, which made it a mega-hit in Japan, Wonder Core and Wonder Core Smart became global hits.

This was my first time visiting his headquarters, located in the business district of Taichung, Taiwan's second largest city. Their 15th-floor offices are modern, open and sleek in design. A large island at the entrance has a wall of fame featuring Wonder Core's most successful products. Outside, overlooking the city, is a balcony large enough for parties.

The office exudes confidence, success and hospitality. Behind the entranceway are two large meeting rooms with glass walls. Eric's office, the president's office, also has glass doors adjacent to his staff's offices. They can see him. He can see them. The spirit of the company feels open, collaborative and connected.

Eric's company had grown from about ten people to 80. He built this organization off his success with OLM. The vibe at his office feels familiar.

Over two days, in addition to discussing his newest business venture, we reminisced.

He brought out pictures of his initial visit to our offices in Japan. He showed me the first time he addressed one of our weekly company-wide meetings. Now, he has weekly company-wide meetings. He recalled conversations he'd had with my staff and me over the course of numerous planning sessions, negotiations and dinners. He noted how our company influenced and inspired him, ranging from the design of his offices to the creation of a company vision, mission and values. And how this led to building a company culture, a focus on truly listening to customers, and the desire to make a meaningful organization that harmonizes two P's: purpose and profit.

Eric shared that he was actively preparing for his company's annual planning meeting, which they modelled on OLM/SJ's annual Kickoff Meeting. He said our company had inspired him. That I, too, had inspired him.

Over dinner, he rehearsed the themes of his speech with me. He believes there are three types of people: people with a dream and a plan; those with a dream and no plan; and others with no dream and no plan. He said he wants to get to know every one of his 80 employees so he can help them define their dreams and build a plan. He feels it is his responsibility to understand them and empower them.

He believes that having a dream and a plan — and the ability to act on both of them — has made him successful, inspired and rich. Now, he wants to give back by empowering the next generation in his company, and he believes that he will benefit, too. It's a virtuous cycle of benefit.

I have tremendous respect for Eric. He was successful before us, but together we achieved great things. One in eight households in Japan purchased a Wonder Core product from us. Our customers loved our products. We made a difference. For him to tell me that I inspired him, that I had made a difference in his life, means a lot to me.

Eric's concept of the three types of people is a Dream Spectrum, and he believes that a dream with a plan is the highest level of self-actualization.

For this book, I want to suggest a modification to Eric's categorization of people. I call it the Purpose Spectrum. I believe there are four levels of the Purpose Spectrum: 1.) People who define a purpose and a plan — leaders; 2.) Those who adopt a purpose to build or follow a plan — inspired and empowered followers; 3.) Individuals with a purpose and no plan — people who feel life offers no opportunity, who are functional but unmotivated; 4.) People with no purpose and no plan — the directionless, who muddle through life without motivation, sense of accomplishment or satisfaction.

This book is a memoir of my journey through all four stages. In my life, I have achieved the most success and satisfaction, both emotionally and financially, when I have been in either stage one or two, when I am focused on purpose and profit, and when I am on the positive side of the Purpose Spectrum.

My 'superpower' is two-fold. I have been a leader, creating purpose and inspiring people to follow me, leading them to serve a greater purpose. And, along the way, we have profited. I have also inspired others to lead, sometimes empowering them within our organization and sometimes outside of it. By creating an expanding circle of purpose-driven leaders and followers, I have benefited financially and spiritually. I say spiritually because I believe we grow as people by serving others. I think it is the healthiest and most satisfying way to make a living.

I am also a fighter. I have fought in the ring, but more importantly, I have fought for a purpose as an individual, a husband, father, brother, business leader, and member of society. Purpose is empowering. It gives us a powerful 'why,' which gives our actions meaning. Purpose is also purposeful. When I endow all of my actions with being purposeful, I have found the greatest success. In the ring, every action must be purposeful. Any non-purposeful action will be exploited and punished.

This book is a chronicle of my fight, recounting how I have learned to find purpose, and live and act purposefully. It is a reflection on how I have fought my way to a certain level of success.

I want to inspire you to identify your place in the Purpose Spectrum. There is a difference between wisdom and experience. Everybody of any age has experience. Whether we are engaged or oblivious, we accumulate experience every minute of every day while we're alive. Wisdom is more meaningful; it is the ability to learn and grow from experience. I know young people with wisdom and old people with a ton of experience but nothing more. Experience without wisdom is empty.

I hope you find some wisdom in my memoir. As noted, I have experienced all four stages of the Purpose Spectrum. I have lived some of the highest highs and lowest lows. I embrace all of my experience. Not everyone is going to be a leader. I have achieved equal measures of success and satisfaction as both a leader and an inspired follower. At some point, we all become leaders or followers. But if we can create or find purpose in everything we do, I believe we all have a fighting chance for success.

BUILDING MY MYTHOLOGY, MY BRAND

Everybody creates their own mythology.

I believe that going through the process of creating that mythology is important. When I was President of Shop Japan, we made our customers the star of their life. It was one of the secrets to our success. My story has good guys and bad guys. It has ups and downs. There is hardship, but it is also a love story. It is a story of defeat and triumph. For you, the reader, my goal is that it is, in the end, a story of hope and optimism; a story, like any good mythology, that is more than entertaining, one that's educating and enlightening.

Branding is part of my story. This mythology is my personal brand, the story where I am the star.

I believe that companies miss this whole aspect of branding; they become so convinced that they are the most important thing. Ultimately, they're not. No matter what the brand is, or the personalities or products underlying it, the brand is the supporting actor in the customers' lives. Brands, like people, often fall in love with themselves. This is not an entirely bad thing, but as a brand or company our mandate should be to empower our customer. As a person, I believe that my highest point of self-actualization is when I have made a difference in the lives of others, even though I am the star of my story.

The other thing about mythology is that, sometimes, it's not entirely true. While I'm not a believer in alternative facts, we all alter our reality to better create our mythology. In my story, we will meet inspiring people who created their reality for good and fraudsters and con men who conjured a reality that almost brought me to ruin. As promised, it is a story with good and bad guys.

The story I will tell is accurate to the best of my knowledge. Now and then, when I talk with friends and share certain stories, they correct me on certain details. I never intended to mislead, but it doesn't matter. Some details may be slightly incorrect or exaggerated, but the core truths are mine.

Socrates said, "Know yourself." This book is the story of my process of coming to truly understand who I am, to understand my strengths in order to exploit them and grasp my weaknesses in order to overcome them. For a fighter, this self-awareness is essential. Nobody is good at everything. The mindset of a fighter — exploiting strengths, defending weaknesses — has guided my life.

I was an English major in college. I seriously considered writing as a career. I never became a writer, but I unleashed my creativity to build businesses and brands, to conquer an industry and to disrupt a country. I didn't write a bestseller (at least not yet) but was part of the creative process that created best-selling products that reached every corner of Japan.

In 2023 I turned 60. In Japan, turning 60 is called *kanreki* (還暦), which roughly translates as 'milestone.' I am writing this book to commemorate this milestone.

My intent is to share my life lessons, my mythology, and my process for approaching relationships, family and business. Think of this as a guidebook. I hope you will laugh and cry with me, learn from my mistakes and be inspired by my successes.

CHILDHOOD

DEAF, DUMB AND BLIND

From the first time I heard the lyrics of The Who's epic rock opera, *Tommy*, I felt a kinship with the boy whose senses shut down after witnessing a murder. The story helped me make sense of something that had happened to me when I was six years old.

I was fidgety. I was dressed up in a suit. It was uncomfortable. I hated wearing it.

Everyone around me was speaking in hushed voices. They told me I was brave. They patted my head and treated me like a fragile object.

I was surrounded by my mother, father, grandmother, uncles, aunts, cousins, friends of all ages. Morissa was just four. The funeral of a child has no joy. There is no celebration of a life lived. There is despair for a life lost. There is anger. There is a loss of hope.

"You're so brave," I heard. "You were such a good brother." Even as a six-year-old, I knew that the words were empty. I didn't want to be brave. I didn't want to be in this place or even know why I was here. I was led to the front of what seemed like a long room, walking by seemingly endless rows of chairs. Everything started to blur and my other senses stopped functioning.

Through the muddle of my mind, I heard, "Harry, Harry, it is time for you to say goodbye." It felt like nobody else was in the room. Just me and a box. A box with an open door. And in front of the door, a set of steps. Steps that I was supposed to climb so that I could look in. I climbed the steps. I was all alone. I was blinded by my surroundings, but all of a sudden I looked in the box and there was my sister, Morissa. She looked just like always, except the hole in her throat to her trachea was closed. She looked fine. But she was dead. She would never wake up. Never grow up. Never smile or play with me again.

She was gone. All alone looking down at my sister, everything went black. I was deaf, dumb and blind. I have no memory of whether I physically ran away in terror or simply ran so far deep into my mind that it had the effect of running away. But that memory is still the scariest moment of my life, one that returns to me in my darkest hours.

This is my oldest memory of figuratively crawling on the canvas in pain. The rest of this story is about how I got back up and started fighting. In my mind, I ran away that day, but it made me stronger.

The complexes of childhood never leave us. Either we learn to overcome them or we are doomed to repeat the same mistakes over and over. Or, more likely, we come to embody a combination of both. Personally, while I constantly struggle with my complexes, I am also thankful for them. They turned me into the person I am today.

There are three personal struggles that have defined who I am today.

I experienced loss.

There was insecurity, rooted in doubts about being good enough and having enough, particularly money.

And I've felt like an outsider.

Losing my sister, my parents' divorce, and constantly moving defined my early life. I was in six different schools between 1st grade and 8th grade. With every move I had to restart. I felt inadequate and confused. When you're a child, you don't understand why people die. You don't understand why your parents divorce. I felt like I had failed. Isn't that too much to put on a young person?

Yet today, I look at every failure — individual, in relationships, in business — as an opportunity to examine what I could have done better. We tell children not to blame themselves for the problems around them, but as an adult, believing that my actions are meaningful has been insightful and empowering.

As a child, there was always a concern about not having enough money. Rightly or wrongly, I associate lack of money with loss and the inability to control one's destiny. My parents' divorce, followed almost immediately by my sister's death. The poverty we lived in immediately after Morrissa died, followed by the constant uprooting and re-starting during my childhood years. This has created a lifelong phobia that I can lose everybody and everything at any time. And that drove me to make money, so that lack of it would never be an excuse for what life threw my way.

With the constant moving I often felt like an outsider. With each move I had to figure out how not to be an outsider.

These three themes — loss, insecurity and the notion of being an outsider — made me who I am today. As a fighter, when I go down from a blow, my mind races with doubt. Slowing down the count, turning doubt into resolve, is one of the lessons I have learned. Fear of loss, fear of not being good enough, and fear of not belonging hardened my resolve to succeed.

It's not as if all I have are bad memories. That's not true at all. But trauma certainly affected my childhood and shaped my life view. It made me stronger and created my unique family situation. By the age of nine, I had four active parents: my mother and stepfather, with whom I lived, and my father and stepmother, whom I'd visit on weekends. I learned from all of them.

My mother had to face terrible fears. I lost a sister, but she lost a daughter.

How do you keep going after losing a child? As an adult, I comprehend better what she gave to me. I learned bravery, optimism, dreaming and creativity. She would look at me and say, "Dream! Don't be confined by the walls." There is abundance in the imagination. We didn't have much for a long time, but my mother never felt that should be an impediment to pursuing our dreams.

But her optimism was always tempered by the pragmatism of my Kansas-born stepfather. And the conflict between dreaming and pragmatism was a constant source of friction between them, ultimately leading to their divorce.

After I left home for university, she redid her whole life. She quit her job as a high school English teacher, became a passionate horseback rider and started a company, Hoofbeats, leading tours of England and Ireland by horseback. She attracted souls who loved horses and needed an opportunity to break from their everyday life. She became their role model, as she had been my role model. She lived the life she preached, and was named *Self* magazine's Woman of the Year.

Through two failed marriages and losing my sister, her ability to create allowed her to rebuild her life. She had undying optimism. Unfortunately, she died early, at 53, of cancer. She never got to see me build on her legacy.

My father was a scholar. He had a passion for knowledge. He was curious about many things and knowledgeable in a diverse set of interests. He had an ability to truly listen. He could not only talk with strangers, but draw them out, appreciate and learn from them. This extended to almost all of the homeless in his neighborhood. He was a passionate patriot. He believed in the premise and the promise of the United States of America. He believed in helping people, providing opportunity and making society better. He was an active, lifelong member of the Democratic Party. We have a copy of an article from the front page of *The New York Times* from 1948, about my father and two other activists being arrested in Georgia for helping black people register to vote. This was pre the civil rights movement!

CHOOSING MY REALITY: TURNING MINUS INTO PLUS

As a child, I started to perceive a new reality. It was three-pronged:

1. Accruing parents and family
2. Learning how to succeed
3. Taking responsibility to make my own money

The birth of my sister, Stephanie, was one of the happiest moments of my life.

My father remarried, to my stepmother, Lyn. At first, I didn't like this change, and I recall that my early relationship with her was quite tricky. I don't remember exactly how and when that changed, but the birth of my sister had a profound impact on me. From the first time I held her, she changed the dynamic of my view of family. Since then, birth has become an essential moment for me. The birth of my brother, my children, my grandchildren, but also the birth of businesses. Against loss, I choose birth.

My mother had also remarried, to my stepfather, Dick. At first, I wasn't happy about him either. Lyn and Dick were intruders; they were preventing me from having my mother and father. But sometime around the gift of having a new sister, my view on all that changed. Rather than my family having been diminished, I chose to view it as enlarged.

Lots of children have had to deal with divorce. I am lucky in that I ended up with four parents, and all four made a difference in my life. They helped shape me and taught me the value of choice. I learned that I had the power to choose my reality, whether to be positive or not. So, loss turned into change, change into accretion. Accruing family brought richness to my life.

Choice is a superpower. It is empowering. It can also be a dilemma. At one time or another, I accompanied all of my parents to religious services, in synagogues, congregational church and the Roman Catholic church. My parents exposed me to their places of worship and left me to choose, which I never did. In my mind, the choice was not about a place of worship but of a parent. After deciding to see my collection of parents as good and unique, I was not willing to choose between them.

My mother became close to my stepmother, notably when Morissa passed away. She was also godmother to my brother and sister. We became an effective but non-traditional family.

During this period, I also learned how to win. As a child, I became really competitive.

I didn't get involved in organized sports until I was in 3rd grade, when I started playing Little League baseball. The previous year I had gone to summer camp, where I learned how to play the sport. They didn't know that I was left-handed, and they gave me all right-handed gear. I would later grow to love baseball, but at first I hated it.

People made fun of me because I couldn't throw or hit. I was the worst player on the team. I was the last person picked. I was the outsider.

When I returned from summer camp, my father invited me outside to toss a ball around. When he saw that I was trying to catch a baseball right-handed, he said, "Why are you doing that? You're left-handed!"

When I first joined the Little League team, I got a glove for my right hand, but for some reason, I still hit from the right side of the plate. I struck out all the time, and I wanted to give up.

One day, I faced a kid on the mound who was the best pitcher in the league. He threw fast but with poor control. He would either strike out or walk everybody. I was the last batter. Our team was losing. We hadn't scored any runs and we didn't have any hits. My nemesis had struck two batters out and walked the bases loaded. My teammates all expected me to be another victim. But I hit the ball. It landed barely fair, near the right-field foul pole. My swing was late and his pitch provided all the power, but this first big hit of my life was a bases-clearing triple.

It would have been nice to hit a home run, but nonetheless, it was a triple! Not bad for the first time I touched the ball with a bat.

This triggered something competitive in me. It changed me. From that point on, whether in baseball or other sports, I decided to become good. Really good. It also taught me the value of competing — of competition as a means of testing myself, learning my weaknesses and strengths, and the value of focused practice to succeed.

And it wasn't just sports. I was also triggered to compete academically, thanks to my 5th-grade teacher, Mr. R.

At that point, school also became a competition. Every week, whoever had the best score on the weekly test would not have to do homework that weekend. And, every quarter Mr. R. would administer 'The Bomb Test,' on all the subjects we had learned. He would award five dollars to whoever had the best score on that exam.

Before 5th grade, I had never cared. To my peers and me, being nerdy wasn't cool. I was a middling student, but given those compelling new incentives, I was motivated to get the best score every time. And I succeeded in winning, pretty much every time! I wasn't a nerd, I was a winner. And I came to believe that winning is cool.

I went from being a mediocre student to one of the best, almost immediately. Economics is about incentives: time and recognition can be as important as money. With the right incentives, people will perform. The free weekends and five dollars every quarter provided the right incentive for me.

On my 10th birthday, I really wanted a ten-speed bicycle with curved handlebars. My parents got me a three-speed mama's-boy bike with straight handlebars. My mother was worried about my posture, and it was also cheaper.

How to express my emotions, my disappointment? I knew they had worked hard to get that bike. I needed to show that I appreciated the gift, but it was not the one I wanted.

I pretended to be happy, but this experience intensified my desire to work so I could make my own money. As soon as I reached the minimum employment age, I got my first job, delivering newspapers. Whether it was bicycles or baseball gloves, if there was something that I truly wanted, I resolved to ensure that I had the power to get it for myself.

Since turning 12, I've always had jobs. My parents still supported me, but I started on the journey of figuring out how to make my own money.

FIGHTING IN THE PLAYGROUND: FINDING A WAY TO BELONG

I got on the service elevator. The regular elevator didn't go to the basement. When the doors opened, I could see the building's furnace in the dim light from a bare bulb hanging from the ceiling. The floor was filthy black. The furnace spouted smoke.

Right after my sister passed away and my parents got divorced, my mother and I lived for a period of time down in that dungeon.

When I came home from school, and entered our apartment building, I would peek left before turning right. On the left was where the superintendent lived. Sometimes the super's son would be there waiting for me. He wanted me to sneak into his apartment with him to watch his parents having sex, although at the time I didn't even know what that meant.

Our apartment was small. The entrance opened to a living room where my mother slept on a fold-out couch. A tiny kitchen held a small table where my mother and I would take our meals. The other room was my bedroom. There was one window that opened into a courtyard where the building's residents deposited their trash. One night an intruder climbed through that window to try to steal what little we had or to molest my mother, or both. The apartment never seemed to have enough light. But maybe that was a result of our mood.

The building was at 96th Street and Lexington Avenue in Manhattan, on the border of Spanish Harlem. The city south of us was posh, but immediately north were progressive stages of poverty. My mother had a very close friend who lived in the luxurious penthouse apartment. We lived in the basement. We lived in lots of places, but this was the worst.

My school was two blocks away. Not even a five-minute walk. I would get off the freight elevator on the ground floor, say hello to the doorman, and leave under the awning of the entrance way. To the left were boutiques, restaurants and ever-nicer upper middle class apartment buildings. To the right was my destination. I crossed the street to a world of pushers, drug users, poverty and my school.

I would eventually learn the rituals of the first day and first week of school, but I remember the first time I made the two-block journey on my own. Sonny was the leader of the reception committee. I don't remember speaking. We just started rolling around on the ground. He was bigger, stronger and surrounded by friends. I just kept fighting. And with Sonny, we never stopped fighting. Whenever and wherever we saw each other, we would continue our frantic embrace for superiority and dominance.

Sonny was my first school nemesis. But not my last. For the next seven or eight years, every school brought a new nemesis. I was the outsider and I arrived knowing that I would have to fight. Every year, at each new school, I had to establish early that I would not be bullied.

I learned three things:

1. That I didn't have to win. The fighting was not about winning but about gaining respect. Playground fights are not to the death. They are to establish boundaries.
2. To be comfortable with being an outsider, while understanding the value of how to recognize and adapt to new environments.
3. How not to hate. I remember once losing control in a fight with a boy who taunted me. Pummeling him made me feel ashamed. Set boundaries and defend. That boy later became my friend.

Fighting on the playground was a fact of life, but they were not real fights. They were rituals. Every tribe has coming of age and acceptance rituals. Fighting on the playground taught me how to quickly learn and adapt to various environments. By necessity and through repetition, this became a skill.

Years later, when I first came to Japan, I was an outsider, a minority. I looked different. I couldn't speak the language. I didn't face a physical fight, although during the 1980s, Yakuza gangsters would sometimes pick fights with us foreigners. Rather, my earlier experiences taught me the group psychology of tribes. Tribes have hierarchies and rituals. This is natural. Entering so many different tribes at an early age showed me that by watching and learning from my surroundings, I would gain entry to the in-group. Tribes create barriers as a defence. As a child, the first ritual was fighting on the playground. I learned how to do it. I learned how not to resent it. As a species, I think we're programmed to protect the group from newcomers. Learning how to probe and break down those defences, in order to enter new tribes, became my skill. On the playground, it was a skill that included my fists.

In Japanese, the word for martial arts, *budo*, combines the characters *bu* (武) and *do* (道). The component "bu" means 'to stop two spears,' and "do" means 'the way.' So, martial arts is the way to stop two spears. I learned this lesson on the playground long before I started practising martial arts. I defended myself and fought to gain entrance and acceptance in the new tribe, but rarely did I hate. As humans we have to learn how to resolve conflict without hate. In my life I've had my share of conflict, but I have very few enemies. There are very few bridges that I've burned, and then only out of necessity.

Human beings are tribal. Tribes have rituals. There is a struggle to enter any tribe. I learned that on the playground. Yet, in today's overprotective world, I don't think many young people get the opportunity to develop these skills. The lesson is truly not *Lord of the Flies*. Even as children, most of the time we figured out how to function without supervision. So I learned to never blame the process. Complaining about the process is a waste of time. I learned to focus on identifying the process and figuring out its mechanics, so that I could succeed.

COMING OF AGE, REBOOT

I didn't have a Bar Mitzvah, but in many ways my 13th year was a coming of age. My mother and my stepfather were both working at the Dwight Englewood School (DES), an elite college preparatory school in northern New Jersey.

I was a faculty brat, so to speak. It triggered a transition, because I had never before stayed in a single school for more than a year and a half. I stayed at DES for five years.

After so much flux, stability was a big change for me. Stability allowed me to gain greater confidence. Ultimately, it also caused restlessness and a longing for the next challenge. This is true for me today.

My mother and stepfather bought a house in Teaneck, New Jersey. My father and stepmother bought a brownstone in Brooklyn.

For the first time, we had roots. Since I'd never lived for very long in any one place, I hadn't developed many friendships that lasted for more than a year.

Being in one place allowed me to create longer friendships, including with one friend who is still close to me today. My experience moving around taught me the skill of developing acquaintances, but I had very few deep friend-ships. This is still true for me today.

The level of education at DES was much higher than anything I'd had before. Since 5th grade, I usually felt like I was the best student in class. At DES, I felt like the dumb-est. I was unprepared for the academic grind.

My 8th-grade history teacher was Ms. O. I believe she gave me a D or an F on my first few tests and papers. I hated her. After a few weeks of watching me flounder, she pulled me aside for mandatory after-school instruction.

She drilled in me a process of organizing and outlining my thoughts. Everything should be organized in sets of three. I should have a thesis or hypothesis, with three points to prove. I should address each point with an additional three points or proofs. I should offer three counter-points to each proof. And I should reach a conclusion. Whether writing a paper or taking notes, she advised me to always organize around point, counterpoint and conclusion.

You may notice in the course of this book that I often revert to three points. If this makes it easier to follow or understand me, thank Ms. O. If not, lay the blame on me.

This was the first school where I didn't have to prove myself with my fists on the playground. I had to learn how to survive in the classroom.

Survival is an instinct and a skill. One of the things I have learned as a fighter is that the human mind and body have a remarkable ability to adapt to stress. How many times have we seen a fighter badly beaten in the early rounds, figure out a way to survive, and somehow the same blows that rocked them earlier in the fight seem less effective later?

If we allow and cultivate our fighting gene, we have a unique ability to learn from stress and get stronger. But first we have to survive the initial shock.

I was floored in my first few months at DES. My fight mechanism kicked in. I wasn't willing to be the worst. So, with my parents' and Ms. O.'s help, I figured out how to first be better and then to succeed.

After figuring out the classroom, I was also able to do team sports. I became captain of the junior-varsity baseball team. There had been a student athlete, Andrew Wenick, who died suddenly of a congenital disease. His parents and the school had set up a scholarship for scholar-athletes in his name. I was awarded the scholarship after my first year at DES.

That was my first public success.

I had overcome my complex of not being good enough. I could compete in the classroom and on the playing field. Most of my peers at DES came from affluent families, so the money gap was a constant source of insecurity. Given that, having a job to generate spending money was now essential.

My most important job during high school was working as a busboy at a high-end steak and seafood restaurant called The Green Dolphin.

My first lesson on the job is one I share with everyone who works for me.

I was standing with my hands in my pockets, pretending to be looking for something to do but probably daydreaming. My boss, Mr. C., came up to me and said, "After I'm done training you, you will never in your life put your hands in your pockets again. There is always something to do!"

He was right. If we have awareness of our environment, there is always something to do.

As a busboy my job was to assist three or four waitresses, who would give me 15% of their tips. Our wage was less than a dollar an hour, so pleasing the waitresses in order to get my share of their tips was critical. Some waitresses lied about how much they received. Learning who to trust and who to avoid became a survival skill.

I competed with the other busboys. Arriving early to get the best area with the best waitresses could result in doubling my take-home pay. Ideally, I would try to be efficient enough to clean and reset tables for four waitresses at a time. That way, I would make $100-120 a day from tips. In the late 1970s and early 1980s, that was good money for a teenager.

Mr. C.'s lessons have never left me. Be aware. No wasted movement. Every movement should have purpose. As a fighter, this mindset is essential. Sometimes you have to keep moving and probing to find opportunity. As a person, being driven by purpose means every hour of the day is meaningful. I've learned to assign purpose to everything I do. Rest, relaxation and play are important. When I'm lying in bed and playing a video game rather than doing something else, it is better and more effective when it is purposeful, rather than idly senseless, which leaves me feeling guilty. Mr. C. taught me to be purposeful in all my actions. That has served me well in the ring. But most importantly, it has served me in life. Thank you, Mr. C.

The second meaningful job I got was in my senior year. The father of one of my classmates ran a chain of gas stations. He created his own brand and decided to expand by selling franchises. He hired my friend and me to do business development. I was 17 years old. I would drive to service stations throughout New Jersey to make presentations on why they should switch affiliation from a major brand to ours. This was my first foray into life as a small business person and an entrepreneur.

At 17, my days would range from having business lunches over martinis to trekking to remote locations in the bowels of industrial New Jersey. I was talking to small station owners, many of whom were deeply unsatisfied with how the major oil companies treated them. We were a small, up-and-coming franchise. We offered an alternative to the big guys, with the potential to make more money and the satisfaction of lifting a middle finger to the rigid structure of major brands. I made several sales. It was great fun.

The Green Dolphin taught me the value of hard work, efficiency and aligning myself with the right people. It taught me that if I keep my eyes open, there is always something to do. My friend's father's business awakened an entrepreneurial spirit. Selling and being part of a business that inspired people was fun.

I was about to leave for college. Being rooted allowed me to gain new skills. I was ready for more.

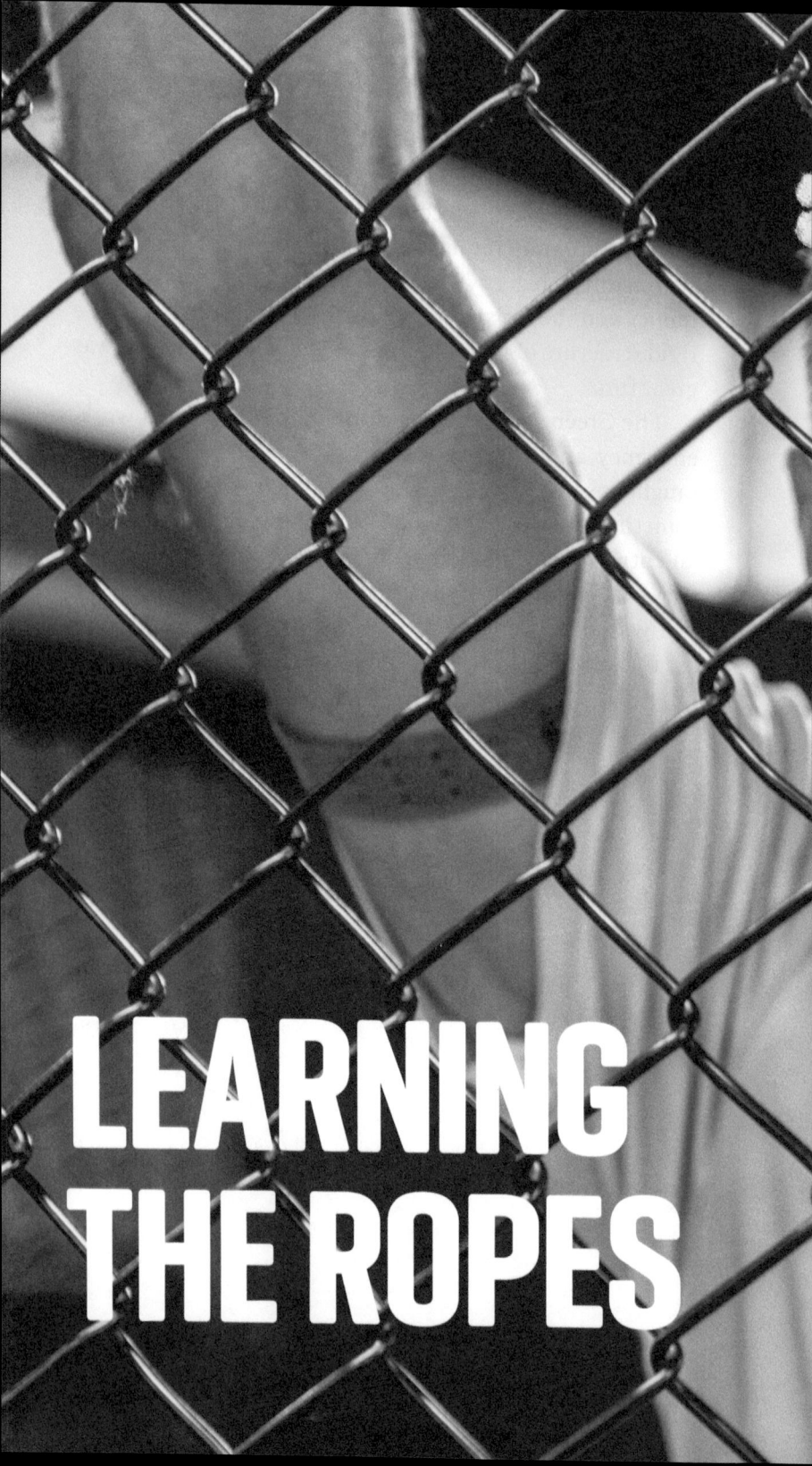

LEARNING
THE ROPES

THE CORNELL YEARS: LEARNING TO SURVIVE IN A BIG POND

At DES, I was successful in the classroom and in sports. I was passionate about baseball, but none of the bigger schools I wanted to attend showed interest in me as a baseball recruit. I was not good enough. I was confronted with a life decision. Stay in a small environment where I felt comfortable and knew I could succeed, or test myself at a bigger venue.

I ultimately chose Cornell University, the alma mater of my birth parents.

I don't recall any pressure from either of them to apply, let alone attend if accepted. So, while they never said I should go there, ultimately it was in my DNA to attend this school in upstate New York. In a subconscious way, it provided me a sense of continuity, of stability. There are signs, or karma, that help govern our lives. My karma was to go to Cornell.

I had achieved success in a small pond. I'd found ways to make a splash. But now I was in a large pond of 35,000 students.

Three key influences that affected my life trajectory emerged when I got to Cornell.

First, once again, I had to learn to compete at a high level, particularly academically.

Second, I was exposed to Shorinji Kempo, a martial art that led to my interest in and subsequent love of Japan.

And third, I identified passions that I would need to sacrifice to move forward. I decided not to be a writer and not to keep playing baseball. One of the great things about Cornell is that it's such a big place and there are so many things to do and different types of opportunities. It was wonderful and overwhelming. As a freshman, I embraced the freedom of living alone for the first time, exploring all the new things I could do, academically, socially, in activities, and in my job as a bartender. Almost inevitably, my first year was a disaster academically.

I'd long had an interest in Asia and martial arts. After the death of my sister, my mother was very protective of me and discouraged contact sports, so I didn't feel free to pursue this interest until I got to Cornell. My fascination with Asia and martial arts also led me to study Chinese. I was looking to be unique in my academic pursuit. Studying Chinese in 1981 was both unique and a colossal mistake!

There were several reasons. Chinese class was every morning at 8.00. As a freshman, getting to class every morning at that hour was not feasible. I missed a lot of classes, and those I attended were often on little to no sleep.

The second reason I did so poorly was that the program wasn't designed for non-native speakers. Of the 80 or so people who started Chinese in the autumn of 1981, I believe only three of us were Caucasian. Everybody else was second-generation Chinese, who already spoke the language to some extent, and took the class to learn how to read and write. The other two Caucasians and I were starting from scratch.

None of us could keep up. At the end of the year, the professor asked me if I intended to continue. I said no.

"OK," she said, "then I will give you a C-minus. If you had said you would continue, I would have had to fail you."

Chinese was one of several less-than-successful courses I took in my freshman year, but I performed well in my humanities classes. I built on those lessons. After that less-than-stellar first year, I believe I made the Dean's List every semester. I began to hone a skill that has been integral to my success: the art of picking the right venue and the right opponent. To succeed in the ring, there is a balance between moving up the ranks and fighting the right fight by carefully picking the suitable weight class, opponent and venue.

As a freshman, I was overwhelmed. I needed to learn how to navigate new challenges. How can I start on a somewhat easier level, but with a clear path to progress?

The most important thing that happened to me at Cornell took place in my first week. Walking through the student center, I saw a group practising a martial art. It was Shorinji Kempo, a self-defense martial art featuring hard and soft techniques. I joined and they became my network, my support group. It was a serendipitous encounter that helped shape my college years and my whole life. Cornell was the only university in the US with a Shorinji Kempo club. Without that encounter, I might not have come to Japan. Karma again.

Our group was quite diverse. The leaders were a mix of postgraduate students and non-students from the local community. In those first few weeks of practice, I made friends and a network that would ultimately open doors. Our club was diverse in age, experience, education and interests. I learned from them. I believe the highest-functioning organizations embrace diversity. Some people might have looked at us as 'different,' but I loved our group and our network.

Some people gravitate to networks or tribes full of people like them. And in college, it's really easy to succumb to that temptation. Encountering Shorinji Kempo was a true turning point in my life. I chose a group that would expand and challenge my life view rather than simply reinforce it. While I no longer practise it regularly, what I learned and the people I met are still part of my life. In my junior and senior years I was co-leader of the group, which helped me develop both my people skills and leadership skills. And, most importantly, Shorinji Kempo led me to Japan.

Each year our group held Camp Cornell, a seminar at a Boy Scout camp in the town of Ithaca, New York. I attended my first Camp Cornell over Memorial Day weekend, following the completion of my sophomore year. Two famous sensei, revered martial arts teachers, came from Japan. I was already passionate about Shorinji Kempo, but this seminar hardened my resolve to make Japan a part of my life. At the end of camp, I broke my wrist in an accident. I was also recuperating from mononucleosis. The sickness and the injury forced me to spend the first two weeks of my summer vacation between sophomore and junior year recuperating.

I couldn't work. I couldn't work out. I couldn't do much of anything. It was probably the longest period of my life in which I really didn't do anything except read and think.

I read *The New York Times* cover-to-cover. It was so clear to me that the world was shifting toward Japan and Asia. To my mind, however, most of the people around me, particularly in the northeastern US, were Eurocentric.

I was already interested in Asia, but I had done miserably in Chinese. I turned my attention toward Japan.

After practising two years of Shorinji Kempo, I had made friends with and grown to respect many Japanese practitioners of the martial art. A deep affection and respect for Japanese people and the country's culture had grown in me.

As I contemplated my future, a clear vision of myself in Japan, making a difference, formed in my mind. News coverage of Japan in the 1980s painted it as the chief competitor to the United States, as a threat. Generally not positive. I read the book *Japan As Number One*, by Ezra Vogel. I became convinced that if I went there, I could become a bridge. I could make a difference in bettering the relationship between the two countries. I resolved to go to Japan.

Prior to that summer, I had been contemplating two career paths: as a writer/journalist or a diplomat. I had pre-registered to study Russian and Russian history. I was already an English major. I had everything lined up to pursue these two possible paths. I thought my course was charted.

I decided to change course.

No one in my immediate circle was preparing for a future in Japan or anywhere else in Asia. I could pioneer my own way. I had a vision to bridge the mighty Pacific.

I announced my intention and took action. I cancelled all the courses for which I'd pre-registered, and in their place signed up for Japanese language instruction, Japanese history and Japanese economics. My parents (all of them) spent the next several months trying to dissuade me. I understood their concerns.

Cornell, one of the eight elite Ivy League schools, was expensive. They were all sacrificing to allow me to go there. In high school I was a good student. The only two subjects that I really didn't do well in were Spanish and Latin. In my freshman year in college I was even worse at Chinese.

My parents argued, "Look, you're just not a good language student. Japanese is the hardest language in the world. This is a bad idea." They feared that I was making a potentially costly mistake, but it hardened my resolve to succeed. When I stayed the course, they changed, too. They eventually came to support me 100%.

I had made key decisions. I was going to find a way to live and work in Japan. I needed to start preparing immediately. Step one was to learn Japanese.

And so, another decision had now been made. I would no longer pursue the study of journalism and writing. This was an important pivot, as I loved literature and was already an English major.

At one point, I had a clear image of myself as a writer. Just as I also once had a clear image of myself as a Major League Baseball player. During the same two weeks as I was thinking about myself in relation to Japan, I recognized that the people who I really respected as writers — William Faulkner, Ernest Hemingway and the like — while tremendous authors, generally lived unhappy lives.

Why should I aspire to live like that?

My focus changed. "I'm going to go make money. I'm going to be happy. It's a choice. And maybe I can write, too." I wanted to keep my creativity, but find ways to create that didn't necessarily involve hardship and pain. In retrospect, I was naive. Creation always involves hardship and pain. I have nursed numerous injuries on my path to success. In the ring or in practice, a little pain is what reminds me that I'm alive. I learn from pain.

Cornell really was a turning point. I was so lucky to be there in the 1980s, because at that time it had the number-one program in the world for learning Japanese. By chance, the only university with Shorinji Kempo also happened to offer the top course for studying the Japanese language. Again, karma. I was in the right place at the right time.

When I started Japanese at Cornell there were a lot of people who had come to the realization that Japan was the wave of the future. So, I guess I wasn't as unique as I'd thought. I was a junior and there were a number of freshmen who started Japanese along with me. Many of them were second-generation Japanese who already spoke the language. But unlike the Chinese class, the Japanese program split them up from the beginners.

Tuition was covered through my parents and student loans. I was busy academically and practising Shorinji Kempo, but I still needed a paycheck. I supported myself at Cornell in various ways. Three of those jobs were the most memorable.

I drove a taxi in New Jersey and New York for about eight weeks. I was a bartender at a university-run bar during my freshman and sophomore years. And one summer I worked as a home health aide.

I learned from all of those activities.

My stint as a taxi driver ended unpleasantly.

I became the pet of the cab company radio dispatcher, Mr. V., an enormously fat man who had to install a barber's chair in the office to support his weight and girth.

He took a liking to me.

Our company was headquartered in Fort Lee, New Jersey, very close to the George Washington Bridge that linked northern New Jersey to uptown Manhattan. When we didn't have a fare, all the drivers needed to be on call, parked on a line at a traffic light overlooking the highway leading to the bridge. When a booking came in, the radio dispatcher would call out: "Who's on the light?" Whoever was first in line would get the fare, and so on. Sometimes the dispatcher would have three or four fares simultaneously and it was clear there was some deference to the older grizzled guys, several of whom were Vietnam veterans. Most of the dispatchers would try to feed those guys first if they had more than one fare to dole out at a time.

But Mr. V. liked me. After a few weeks, it became clear to everyone that he was feeding me. He would call, "Who's on the light?" in rapid succession. The first fare would be to take an old lady to the supermarket: a $2.50 fare. The second fare might be slightly more lucrative, but local. And then I'd be on the light, and lo and behold, my fare would be a roundtrip airport fare, which would be in excess of $40-50 each way, usually with a generous tip.

Mr. V. expected me to work long shifts. Over the course of that summer, I was often driving 12-hour days, from 7 am to 7 at night, five or six days a week.

My fixed hourly rate was less than $1 an hour. At the end of each day, I would pay 60% of what I had generated on the meter back to the company, and keep my tips. With Mr. V. feeding me, I was a money-making machine over those eight weeks.

I made close to $15,000 in cash.

Making money was important to me, but it was also becoming a sort of phobia, in part amplified by a rock song.

At some point during the summer, I had a nightmare. In the dream, I was driving my taxi and the song *Money*, by Pink Floyd, came on the radio.

In the dream it was night, and another car suddenly crashed into me, and I knew I was going to die. I woke in a cold sweat, thinking that I could die in the pursuit of money. It's a nightmare that has recurred several times since.

My last interaction with the obese Mr. V. happened near the end of the summer. Since our shifts usually ended at around the same time, he would ask me to drive him home. I was young and naive. He was being extremely good to me. I never thought anything of it.

The last time I drove him home, he asked me to help carry several boxes up to his apartment. Of course, I did so, as he would struggle to carry his own weight up the stairs.

The apartment was depressing, with drab colors and over-sized furniture to accommodate this ugly, grossly over-weight man. When I finished bringing the boxes to his living room, he came up and tried to fondle me from behind. He whispered in my ear that he had taken care of me and how he could continue to do so. After months of him 'feeding' me, he expected payback.

I had grown up fighting on the playground. I had accepted and learned about tribal rituals. But this was not a ritual. This was self-defence pure and simple. While I still had a long way to go in my study of martial arts, he was not a physical match for me. Ultimately, his main attack was psychological. I owed him, and he, who held the purse strings, would give me more. I pushed him away and left. He told me never to set foot in the cab company's office again. I never did.

We've all heard the phrase 'nothing is free.' I lived that lesson. And I walked away unscathed. Lucky to have fended off a predator, but also stronger and more confident. And $15,000 richer.

Although I only drove a taxi for two months, I have a multitude of stories that I still share with people. The first and only time I had a gun drawn and pointed at me. Acting as the chauffeur for a well-dressed, polite gentleman who was probably running drugs. Delivering high-end call girls to waiting clientele. In retrospect, all funny stories, but all learning experiences, imparting formative lessons that I carry with me to this day. And despite the fact that I value what I learned, they are experiences I never wanted my children to recreate. Had my parents known at the time, I'm sure they would not have allowed me to continue. Yes, there was risk. But just as in the ring, I learned from risk.

The other legacy from that time was a severe aversion to Pink Floyd, particularly the song *Money*. I have only recently overcome my Pink Floyd phobia, and regret that I missed out on listening to their music for the last 40 years.

For my first two years of college, I worked 2-3 nights a week during the academic year as a bartender.

As it was a college bar, we'd have to ask everybody for an ID card to verify their age.

I found that learning someone's name and birthday, right from the first interaction, gave me a great head start in striking up a friendship. That's especially beneficial when it comes to talking with women. So, amid being busy with studies and work, the bartending job also added to my social life. It was a great release.

Finally, I spent one summer as a home health aide. Initially I was assigned to work with older people, some of whom were dealing with end-of-life issues.

But in the last four weeks, I was assigned to help a teenage boy. He was 14 years old, so only a few years younger than me. He had been hit by a car when he had tried to cross a busy highway, and ended up with multiple fractures in his legs. At first they weren't sure if he was going to survive, keep one of his legs or walk again.

But he did. He was going through a painful recuperative process and was very depressed. His parents were concerned about him. He was on a suicide watch list. He thought his life was over and that he would never be able to do the things he loved again.

He and I connected. He told me that he loved fishing, but thought he'd never fish again. His home was only a block and a half away from a pond. He had a raft, and prior to the accident he'd spent days fishing from it out on the pond. So, I asked his parents if it was OK to take him fishing. They agreed, but said they didn't think it would be logistically possible. I figured out how to use his wheelchair to first transport the raft to the pond. Then I would get him. I would get him in the raft and we'd fish together for 2-3 hours a day. Then I would reverse the procedure to get the wheelchair, the boy and the raft back home.

News got out about our fishpond excursions. My company featured me in their monthly magazine. I was the aide who helped his charge not only recuperate, but regain his desire to live.

The most rewarding moments of my career have come when there is a clear and meaningful purpose. When my teams and I have been most purpose-driven, we have achieved the best results. We've made a difference in people's lives and have made money. My short stint as a young home health aide started me on the road to this understanding. I could make money and I could make a difference. And I made a difference because I didn't just do what was expected; I was driven to exceed expectations. Everyone benefited. I would need to learn this lesson several more times before it really sank in.

BIG IN JAPAN: BECOMING A STAR IN GIFU

I had two years to prepare for my big move to Japan. I had become goal-focused and set my priorities.

I recall a conversation I had with a woman who showed an interest in me. I was interested too, but I said to her, "Look, I'm interested, but you have to understand that right now my priorities are: number one, studying; number two, Shorinji Kempo, because that's my ticket to Japan; and number three would be you. Are you OK with that?" And it worked. I was amazed. In fact, it worked with several women, and they would start going to Shorinji Kempo with me. Unfortunately, my dojo-mates became frustrated by the various women who would start with our group but then fade away when our relationship fizzled out.

I was singularly focused on getting to Japan. I applied for a position with the Japanese government as a Monbusho English Fellow, which sent native English speakers to prefectural boards of education.

It was 1985, and I was among 59 people hired for the positions. I was assigned to Gifu Prefecture, a district in central Honshu, Japan's main island. When I first heard

I was being stationed there, I was disappointed. The head-quarters of Shorinji Kempo was in Shikoku, a southern island in the Japanese archipelago, so I wanted to be near there. There was scant information available about Gifu, so I didn't know what I was walking into. But in retrospect, once again I was in the right place at the right time.

In Gifu I experienced things, learned many lessons and formed relationships that continue to influence my life and my business. It was there that I met Yumiko, who would become my wife and with whom I'd build a family. And I went from being an outsider to being a Gifu-jin, a person of that place. I believe in fate and karma. Fate brought me to Gifu.

Gifu at the time was off the normal Japan track. For someone like me, being in a region with no other non-Japanese people was lonely, isolating and ultimately a bless-ing. I would sometimes go weeks at a time without seeing another Caucasian.

In those early days, I made three resolutions to myself.

First: master the language. Without that, I could not see a path to success in Japan.

Second: learn how to blend with the culture. Shorinji Kempo was a very important part of that. Meeting and falling in love with Yumiko was even more important. And, yes, she started practising Shorinji Kempo, too. In fact, since Shorinji Kempo is a registered Zen-based religion in Japan, we had one of our sensei conduct our marriage ceremony.

Third: create a network of contacts and friendships. This would be the springboard for my future.

But first, I had to survive my first six months. I was lonely, isolated. I was living in a run-down teacher's hous-ing complex. My apartment had no hot water, no shower. Every evening I would fill the bathtub and then use a port-able heater to heat the water. I would bring the water to almost boiling in the evening, so that it would still be hot in the morning for my bucket-brigade shower. My toilet was a traditional squatter, but it was so small that I hit my knees against the opposite wall as I squatted down.

Those were creature discomforts. My balcony over-looked a small cemetery that was surrounded by rice fields. These rice fields would almost defeat my dream.

From childhood, I suffered from severe allergies and asthma. Unbeknownst to me, I was allergic to blooming rice. I arrived in Japan on 26 June, and by the time the rice crop was getting near to harvest in September and October, I had lost the ability to breathe. I ended up spending a week in the hospital with severe bronchitis. My employers wanted to send me back home.

Yumiko and I had first met in August. When my health started to fail, she found a hospital that would treat me. She would visit me every day to cheer me up, to make sure I didn't lose my will to succeed. Her smile, as it would so many more times in my story, would light my world when darkness crept in. Without her, I wouldn't have made it through those first six months.

But I did. After I got out of the hospital, the board of education still wanted to send me home. They were worried. They made me promise not to get sick again. But I had three goals, and I would not be deterred.

Prior to arriving in Japan I was a relatively disciplined person. I now became more disciplined. During my first two years in Gifu, I was tasked with visiting schools around the prefecture. I was often commuting 60-90 minutes each way.

I made a rule. While I was commuting, I would allow myself to do one of two things: study Japanese or sleep. If I studied the language for too long, I would fall asleep, so I had to give myself two options. That way, I wouldn't constantly feel like I was failing.

I made this rule after I got out of the hospital in October 1985. At the time, I was minimally capable in Japanese. Less than two years later I was conversant. I would continue to improve, but by the end of my second full year in Japan, I was able to make friends and, most importantly, do business in Japanese.

I taught myself the *kanji*, or Japanese characters, using James Heisig's book, *Remembering the Kanji*. The book was exceptional because it introduced a methodology that made learning *kanji* dramatically easier. In less than a year, I learned more than 1,800 characters of the Toyo word list, the number of *kanji* officially recognized by the Japanese government. Finding the most efficient way to train my mind or body, finding hacks — those helpfully creative workarounds — has become a lifelong obsession.

Second, I was learning how to blend with the culture. My involvement in Shorinji Kempo was invaluable. From my first day at the dojo, I had friends with a shared passion. While my actual vocabulary was still quite limited, we could communicate through the language of our shared passion.

Shared passions transcend conventional language. Shared passions and values allow for communication, even if language itself is lacking. They also allow for entrance into the tribe.

When I first came to Japan, I often resented it when random people would ask me, "Can I practise English with you?" I would reply, "That's the wrong question! What do you want to talk about? Be interested in me as a person, not as an object to meet your needs. If you're just going to ask me random questions, I'm going to get bored in two or three minutes. So, be interesting to me. Then let's have a conversation." I wanted engagement. I did not want to be merely an object that someone bounced their well-practised English words off.

I think one of the reasons that English education in Japan is ineffective is that it fails to allow people to focus on and explore their passions. Pursuing passions is active. Learning a language must be, too.

Exploring passions is a theme of my life and one of the ways I've achieved success in marketing and other areas of business. People are people. Passions — and personal complexes, those tangles of emotions, memories, perceptions and wishes — know no borders. Finding people with shared passions opened up my network of friends and contacts. One of those friends became my wife! She joined Shorinji Kempo and practised with me, without much verbal communication at first, but things developed from there.

My biggest passion was the blossoming relationship with Yumiko. We learned to communicate. We shared a passion for laughing, being outdoors, and Shorinji Kempo. She introduced me to her friends and made me feel at home.

I learned that in order to blend with a tribe, I needed to understand the points of pleasure and pain. Expanding my understanding of shared values enabled me to create lasting relationships, where differences like race, gender and age stopped being a hindrance. I started perfecting this craft in the dojo in Gifu. This represented a small but meaningful sample size. Over time, I would use this same mindset to market megahit products throughout Japan. My experience in that small pond became my treasure trove.

I was starting to appreciate the value and the art of networking.

After spending two years as an English teacher, I was appointed the first Coordinator for International Relations (CIR) for Gifu. My appointment coincided with the prefecture's preparations to host Mirai-Haku, a regional expo that turned out to be one of the most successful in the history of Japan.

Working on the Mirai-Haku planning committee allowed me to gain new experience and expand my network beyond my colleagues at the Board of Education and dojo-mates. Again, I was in the right place at the right time. Being a CIR in Gifu from 1987 until the completion of the expo in the fall of 1988 actually made me something of a local celebrity.

Mirai-haku was the first regional expo in Japan that would have an English name, and the organizers asked me to come up with it. It would become known as 'Future Watch 88.' They made a big deal of the English name in the media. Originally, as CIR I was supposed to work in the prefectural office. The leaders of the planning committee pushed to have me work full-time with them. The goal was to put Gifu on the map.

When I arrived in 1985, I was the only Westerner working for the Gifu government. By 1987, there were more than 20 of us. As the person with the longest tenure, I often acted as the leader of our group. I had come to love everything about Gifu, but the dearth of information about the area bothered me. So, I organized a number of us to write a two-book set called *Gifu in the Heart of Japan*. One volume was about the area's people, culture, business and natural beauty, and the other a guidebook. My prefectural bosses loved the idea and gave us a budget. I pushed things along on a tight deadline, so the material would be published prior to the opening of the expo. We made it happen. In a small rural prefecture in Japan that didn't make hasty decisions, the power of a dream, passion and initiative made this project happen.

My wedding became a media/political event. Since I was working for the government, when my bosses found out that I was getting married, several invited themselves to the ceremony, including local politicians, a former Japanese Cabinet member and the governor-elect.

As Yumiko and I were greeting our guests, two newspapers and a TV station covered the reception line. This was not simply a marriage between Yumiko and me, but a symbolic union of Gifu and the United States. Several of the politicians insisted on giving speeches, with English interpretation, prior to the toast. They spoke on the dais with the American and Japanese flags in the background. Our wedding reception was supposed to run two hours. The pre-toast speeches alone took 90 minutes!

When I first learned I was being sent to Gifu, I was disappointed. The little I was able to learn about the place gave me no clue to what wonderful experiences I would have. I came to this far-off place, and I made a difference. I became a big fish in a small pond. I had set three goals and I achieved them. And, most important of all, I met my wife.

As a fighter, choosing the right opponent and weight class is essential. Creating an environment to challenge yourself and refine your skills is essential. It is a process of development. Going too challenging too soon can be catastrophic. Not challenging yourself can lead to complacency. I had passed the challenge presented to me in Gifu.

I was ready for something new.

"GREED IS GOOD": MY TIME ON WALL STREET

I had been in Japan for three and a half years and had achieved my goals: I'd mastered the language, learned to adapt to Japanese society and culture, and had a network of friends and advocates who would help me in the future. In fact, several of them would eventually become business partners. And I was married. That had not been on my list, but I had found a life partner.

What can I say about Yumiko? Although this is my story, it is also her story.

At her 60th birthday I told our gathered family and friends that the first thing that attracted me to Yumiko was the radiance of her smile. She had a smouldering positive energy. She radiated it the first time we met and it hasn't changed in the almost 40 years we've known each other. We have both changed, evolved, but Yumiko's brightness is constant.

She has always believed in me and had unwavering faith that things would work out. Even in the darkest of times in business, or when my mother died, Yumiko has been a constant. And frankly, I have been her biggest supporter as well. She is a free spirit. She is outgoing, vociferous and unconventional, in a country that often represses people who are different. We accepted each other. We have each made the other successful. We are strong individually. We are stronger together.

But even with her by my side, after three and a half years, I needed a break from Japan. After being immersed in Gifu, I felt disconnected from the US, my family and American culture. I had even started to stutter when speaking English.

My first years in Japan were before the advent of the internet and email. International calls were expensive, so it was difficult to keep in touch with my family and friends. I missed them.

Yumiko and I moved back to the States. Right before our move, in 1988, I had seen the movie *Wall Street*. Gordon Gecko's mantra, "Greed is good," stuck in my mind. I didn't want to cheat anyone, break the law or go to jail, but I wanted to be rich.

I decided to try my hand on Wall Street. I interviewed with several companies. None of the US firms were hiring, but I ended up with two job offers, one from a regional bank headquartered in Gifu, and the other from a Japanese securities company, introduced to me by a former colleague in Gifu. I wanted to work on Wall Street, but I was also interested in earning an MBA. I chose to enter Yamaichi Securities as a sales trader for US securities because they said that half of my job would be working on the trading floor and the other half would be business training. As in Gifu, I would be paid while developing new skills. This seemed like the perfect solution.

I quickly realized that what sounded too good to be true was in fact not true. I was a sales trader. I helped facilitate transactions between our bond traders and Japanese institutional clients, mostly banks and life insurance companies. I was working at an entry-level job. The pseudo business school training never came about. We never had the time.

I never received the formal training that had lured me to the position in the first place. Nonetheless, my short stint on Wall Street taught me lessons that are still valid today.

I learned not to be afraid of money.

I'd never had a lot of money. Working as a teacher in Gifu, money was adequate but not plentiful.

As a sales trader of bonds, my first responsibility in the morning was to assist the repo desk, which buys securities with an agreement that the seller will repurchase them at a later time. Between about 7 and 9 am, before the market opened, Japanese banks would call us to borrow anywhere from $500 to $1 billion in treasury bonds. We would typically lend $2-3 billion in treasuries every morning. These trades were usually for a single day. The banks would examine their asset requirements every morning and borrow the treasuries from us if they had a shortfall.

The repo market closed when the market opened. During the day, I was the conduit for day trades between our Japanese institutional clients and our bond traders. For the day trades, the minimum trade was $1 million, or 'one unit.' Each tick upward or downward was ⅛ of a point, which equated to $12,500. Generally, our trading desk and our clients took positions and closed positions every day. I was the most junior of three members on the Japanese institutional sales team. On most days, between the three of us, we would facilitate $150-200 million in sales, although on some days the number could be much higher.

On my second day I made a mistake in Japanese. I said five-eighths when I meant to say one-eighth. Before I could correct myself, the client on the other end of the phone said, "Done." Our bond traders essentially played an arbitrage game every minute of every day. When I asked our trader to 'bid a bond,' that meant I was asking on behalf of my client how much our trader would be willing to pay for

$1 million worth of the 30-year treasuries. In this instance, he said something like 100⅛. That probably meant he already had a different client he would immediately sell the bond to at ⅜, thus securing a $12,500 arbitrage for our firm. He said ⅛. I said ⅝. My client said OK. I had locked in a loss of ⅜ of a point, or $48,500. Just slightly less than my entry-level annual salary. Of course, it was a huge snafu. Several different layers of colleagues and management took their turns yelling, screaming and cursing me out. Within 15 minutes it was forgotten. This was a perpetually quick-turnaround business. We had to move on to the next trade. We had to make our money back.

Learning to rapidly work through calculations was tremendously important. I had to learn how to quickly calculate profit and loss on each transaction. This was before AI or computer trades. We were dependent upon the speed of our minds. Today, so much is automated. Traders now rely on tools with lightning-fast response time. But almost every successful businessman I have ever worked with or studied, from my future business partner Robert Roche to Elon Musk, has an ease and facility with computing numbers and knowing if they feel wrong or right.

I learned not to be intimidated by the sum.

Most importantly, in a short period of time, Wall Street taught me what I didn't want to do. I didn't want to work on Wall Street. This is a lesson I have shared with young people for years. We have stages in our careers. In our 20s, I think it is invaluable to experiment. It's important to find purpose and passion. But when we are younger, the process of elimination is just as important as deciding on the one thing. I was able to identify a career that I didn't want for myself. From a purely statistical perspective, it is unlikely that one's first choice of career will end up becoming a lifelong pursuit. Wall Street wasn't for me.

There were several important reasons why I didn't want to stay in this first career, which were leading me to learn more about myself.

The trading floor was a high-stress environment. I looked at the people around me. Everyone who'd been there for more than 12 months had thinning hair, poor complexion, was overweight, smoked and looked altogether unhealthy. The firm hired beautiful women to walk the floor, providing clerical assistance and visual motivation to keep the testosterone running high.

Some of the people around me were getting rich, but at what cost? Was this truly the best place for me to try to make my fortune? It appeared to be a Faustian bargain: money in exchange for years of my life. Was this the best I could do?

And if I did make this choice, what was the purpose other than money? How would I be growing and evolving as an individual? How would I be making the world a better place? The journey for me to fulfil my potential and make a difference in the world seemed long and uncertain.

When I was in Gifu, whether it was teaching or working for Future Watch 88, our actions were driven by purpose. I jumped out of bed in the morning. I was having fun. I was making a difference. I could see the difference on the faces of the people I interacted with.

In bond trading, I was just a cog, a part. I had no sense that I was making the world a better place. I felt a heaviness in my limbs every morning. I couldn't wait for the day to end. I had faceless clients on the other end of the phone, and we were more likely to curse each other than to share a drink and a laugh. It was, quite simply, an 'I win and you lose' proposition, endlessly repeated.

Working on the trading floor at Yamaichi Securities was one of the few times in my life when I worked in a pure win-lose environment for a sustained period of time. There was no camaraderie, no friendship. Either we made money or lost money. We kept score every day. We looked for little advantages. We looked to take advantage of misstatements or mistakes, like what happened to me on my second day. Our only purpose was profit. That was not a purpose that made me want to go to work every day. That purpose brought me no joy.

I wanted to make money. But I needed something deeper, too.

I made the decision to quit. This was a difficult call. Yumiko and I had moved halfway around the world. While I hated my job, I loved being around and reconnecting with my family. But I had chosen the wrong place, doing the wrong thing. I was not motivated to win this fight.

It was 1989, right after the Black Monday market crash, a time of great uncertainty. Wall Street wasn't hiring. The job market was tight. People kept telling me how lucky I was to have gotten a job when nobody else was able to. But it just wasn't right for me.

People talk about having the courage to start. I think the decision to quit and change course often requires even more courage. I quit. I worried that people could interpret this as a failure, and I could be seen as weak. But I had started to feel empty. Dead. I needed to be alive again.

In many ways, my time on Wall Street proved to be a valuable life experience. I learned to be more comfortable with money. I learned that I needed purpose. I learned to not fall victim to the sunk cost fallacy — that tendency to stick with an endeavor even after it's clear that the costs outweigh the benefits — and summon the courage to walk away when I realized future returns would be low. All three lessons made my time on Wall Street the education I needed, although not the one that I had envisioned.

BACK IN JAPAN: REALIZING PROFIT AND PURPOSE WITHOUT SUSTAINABILITY

After less than 18 months in the US, Yumiko and I returned to Japan. We felt there was more opportunity there than in New York. I had three new themes.

First, I had to have a dream. And, more importantly, I needed a sense of purpose.

Second, I was becoming increasingly aware of my surroundings. I was in my mid-20s, but already numerous opportunities seemed to flash in front of me. I could sense that I needed to develop the skill of grabbing at opportunity when it presented itself and retreating quickly when circumstances changed.

And third, there was what I call my 'jumping ponds' strategy.

During my three and a half years in Gifu, I had been a star, but during my year on Wall Street I was nobody. New York at the time was still reeling from Black Monday, whereas Japan, at least officially, was booming. I felt it offered more chances to succeed than where I was. If the opportunities were in Japan, why was I in New York? Clearly, I was in the wrong pond.

In September of 1989, I resigned from Yamaichi. I had no plan yet. Then fate intervened. On the day I quit I received a call from someone I had met in Gifu during the Future Watch 88 expo.

Dave Wilkey is a Mormon from a small town in Utah. I'm a New Yorker. We should have been like oil and water, but from the first day we got to know each other, we were kindred spirits. We shared a passion to make money, but tempered by the desire to give back to our families, our friends, our immediate society. Our shared values and sense of purpose transcended our different backgrounds.

Dave had brought youth performing groups to Japan for cultural exchange in Gifu as part of our internationalization efforts for the expo. At the time, he and I had vaguely discussed the idea of starting a business. And now, he was calling because he was convinced the opportunity was real and immediate.

Japanese municipalities, primarily from the Chubu region, were contacting him because they wanted to host performing groups similar to those we had staged at Future Watch 88. The hosting institution would provide homestays, venues and sightseeing. Promoting international exchange, particularly grassroots international exchange, or *kokusai kouryu*, was all the rage in Japan. Dave could find the groups who wanted to come to Japan. He needed someone on the ground to handle all the logistics and find more local partners. He needed someone with my skills; he needed me.

We spent several months working out the details. He became my first business partner. We are still partners and, more importantly, friends.

Organizing grassroots exchange opened up numerous opportunities. In addition to junior performing groups, we started to diversify. We put together the first trip to Japan by Legends in Concert, which later became an ongoing act at Universal Studios in Osaka. We established the first horseshoe pitching competition and exchange in Japan.

Friendships were built and sister city agreements were signed that continue to this day. From 1990-1996, we facilitated visits by thousands of people between Japan and the US. We helped create friendship and goodwill. We made a difference and we made a living.

My time in Gifu and the network I had built there made me uniquely qualified to capitalize on the grassroots exchange boom. Many of the people in the local municipal governments in and around Gifu Prefecture either knew me or knew of me. In Japan, precedent, or *jiseki*, is valued highly. At the expo we had set a precedent with homestay and performing groups to create successful relationships. Between this accomplishment and the assistance of my friends and professional network, we built a business.

JUMPING TO A BIGGER POND

While my experience and network in Gifu was the catalyst, as I was preparing to relaunch, I knew I needed to be in yet a bigger pond. While there was opportunity there, it was still a small pond.

Over the years, I have developed a business philosophy around becoming a big fish in a small pond and then jumping to a bigger pond. Yumiko and I jumped south from Gifu to neighboring Aichi Prefecture, which we felt was the biggest pond near Gifu. It was a deliberate choice. I could leverage my existing network, but with more breadth.

Whenever possible, especially when creating a business, I've tried to start in areas with less competition. I try to find a niche, whether it is a place, a product or a service. I focus on succeeding on a smaller stage before trying to compete on a bigger stage. In 1990, Nagoya was the third largest metropolitan area in Japan, the center of the Chubu region, and home of automotive giants Toyota and Honda. It was a big pond in many ways, but we were the first private company there looking to capitalize on the huge interest in the *kokusai kouryu* cultural exchange movement.

Dave had raised some capital, enough for about four months of operations. Yumiko and I knew we would need to bootstrap. We plunged in.

We hit the ground running. Several local governments had already contacted Dave. I started from there. We focused on international exchanges, but our main goal was to search for opportunities. We started by creating grass-root events, but the real currency was creating friendships.

Japan was still a closed society in the 1990s. Most people, even successful business people, especially outside of Tokyo, didn't have contacts and networks with non-Japanese people. Particularly in the Chubu region, the spread of internationalization to the everyday person was glacial. This dearth of access and information created glaring inefficiencies. By going niche and solving the information deficit I was able to create a business and make a living.

As I said, our first businesses focused on bridging this information gap for international exchange, which quickly morphed into travel as well. I also identified opportunities in sports representation, and real estate and relocation services.

I have learned that a successful entrepreneur is rarely the inventor. More often, he or she is the person who either finds inefficiencies and solves them, or is first or best at monetizing an idea. Or they do both.

Access to information for travel and cultural exchange was an inefficient market. The major travel companies had a monopoly on travel services. They were expensive and inflexible. Local governments were yearning for more access to international exchange. Creating sister-city relationships or similar types of linkages was all the rage. The major travel agencies acted as the gatekeeper. We saw an opportunity to open up the gate.

At the time, during the bubble years, the municipal governments, particularly in the Chubu region, also had a budget to pursue this type of exchange. The governments were outsourcing the process of finding suitable partner cities in the US to the big travel companies, who were charging a tremendous margin without really putting the two parties together. We saw an opportunity to create deeper relationships, provide better value and make money. That was my first business.

At the time, the major tour companies would organize 13-day study trips for municipalities. The package would often run in excess of ¥500,000, or around $3,300.

Air travel was more expensive than now, but usually no more than a ¥150,000 (roughly $1,000) round-trip. Dave and I were hired to handle the ground package, with an emphasis on building relationships. We would charge around ¥150,000. So, the whole package cost was ¥300,000 ($2,000) or less, but the governments were paying ¥500,000 per person. Similarly, when we brought groups to Japan, the travel agencies were charging the local governments a fee to organize the groups and charging our groups for homestay in Japan. They were taking money from both sides, but leaving most of the work to us.

First we focused on creating meaningful contacts, exchange and friendship between our US and Japanese organizations. Then we cut out the gatekeeper. We sold our ground packages directly to the local governments. And we set up the events in Japan directly. We lowered the cost for the local governments and the participants.

By creating relationships, we were able to build a business around reciprocal visits. Once or more per year, a group from Japan would visit their partner city or school in the US. Conversely, once or more per year the US side would visit Japan. We helped foster relationships and friendships that continue today. We also created additional value by streamlining the process. From 1990-95 we brought up to

1,000 people a year in each direction. We had fun. We made money. We created an enormous amount of goodwill.

Dave had a friend who had co-founded the Japanese subsidiary of a US network marketing company. They had grown to more than $500 million in annual sales. They hired our group to run the domestic packages for their semi-annual incentive tours, and our services were well received. The company credited us with helping to increase the motivation of their distributors, which in turn helped them grow.

Again, we saw that the large travel companies were making enormous margins, while we were providing the content at a relatively low cost. We negotiated with the client to allow us to create a special tour and to negotiate directly with the airlines on their behalf. We were able to reduce the client's cost by approximately ¥100,000 per passenger, while at the same time almost tripling our profit margin. At its peak, we were taking 2,000-2,500 Japanese to the US.

Japan was still in the throes of the bubble. The local governments, corporations and everyday people were confident and flush with money. The travel system at the time was closed and anachronistic, which allowed us to step in as disruptors and provide more service and a better experience at a lower cost. We were clearly providing value.

It was a great business. It was a niche. It fulfilled a purpose. It was profitable. The process of identifying and exploiting an inefficiency was a valuable experience. It is an experience I have repeated. The heady days of the bubble finally burst in 1995-96, and so did the budgets of local governments and schools to mount exchange programs. The international exchange merry-go-round kept going, but much more slowly. The salad days lasted only five years in all. Japan ultimately reformed the travel system to allow operators to provide low-cost, low-margin packages.

The inefficiency in the system got corrected. The value and margins in providing an alternative to package tours disappeared. We still had a business. We continued to offer high-touch, experiential travel packages, but our margins were dramatically reduced. Our deep-value, highly-profitable business proved unsustainable. It became a normal business — not bad, but not the venture that would change my life.

International exchange and travel supported me for the first several years after I came back to Japan. The contacts I made running this business helped plant new seeds of opportunity. These bloomed quickly, but their life cycle was relatively short. This was also the first business I ever sold, for the modest sum of ¥10,000,000. At the time, it seemed like a great amount of money.

SITTING DOWN WITH LEGENDS

While I was active in running my first business, I dabbled in the field of sports representation and marketing.

In the early 1990s, Japanese baseball teams did not recognize sports agents. Players in Japan negotiated directly with the teams for their contracts. Hideo Nomo winning freedom from his contract and ultimately signing with the Los Angeles Dodgers started the fall of this system. But during the bubble years, US agents wanted access to Japan for sports talent, particularly players who were either languishing in the minors or unable to break into the starting lineups of a major league team.

I had become friends with a retired player who had been the first to come directly from the US majors to play for a Japanese team. After retiring, he had also managed two American teams, so he had deep ties in both US and Japanese baseball. I met him at a hotel restaurant in Nagoya in late 1990 and we immediately hit it off. He was scouting players for a couple of Japanese teams. He introduced me to their agents, who then hired me to represent their players in Japan. In this way, I was the first (or one of the first) quasi-sports agents in Japan.

In addition to representing talent, we brainstormed ideas to bring US Major League baseball and Japanese baseball closer. I learned a key lesson from one of our ideas: with a powerful and compelling story, I could find a way to walk through any door.

We put together the first Japan-US Baseball Friendship game. My friend told me how much the athletes who had played in Japan wanted to come back. Unlike in the US, there were few opportunities for these old timers to appear before their fans. We were able to convince about 20 of the most famous foreign players to star in Japan to agree to come over for expenses and a small fee. We had a team. We needed an opponent and sponsors.

We approached the Meikyukai (the Golden Players Club), a rival Japanese Hall of Fame and non-profit organization created by Masaichi Kaneda, the most successful pitcher in Japanese baseball. Any player with 2,000 or more career hits or 200 or more career wins became a member. They were the perfect opponent for our All-Star team.

The challenge was how to get the Golden Players Club to embrace the idea.

My friend was acquainted with Sadaharu Oh, the Japanese Home Run King, and brokered a coffee meeting.

I was a 28-year-old kid, a huge baseball fan, pitching this idea of a friendship game between Japanese Hall of Famers and my team of ex-players from the US. Oh not only gave me the time of day, he said, "OK, come back next week. I want you to meet the director and some of my colleagues at the Golden Players Club."

The following week I arrived at the club's office in a building in the Ginza, Tokyo's upmarket shopping district, where 20 years later Oak Lawn Marketing (OLM) would also have an office. I walked in and Oh greeted me and introduced me to the non-profit's executive director, who I was expecting to meet, and to my surprise also Masaichi Kaneda and Shigeo Nagashima. I was now sitting down with the three most famous players in the history of Japanese baseball.

There are people all over Japan who would kill for the opportunity to meet these legends. Over coffee, I presented my idea. When I finished, they turned to the executive director and said, "We should do this. Let's see if we can find a sponsor."

I won't go through all the details, but suffice to say that the event happened. Two games were held at the end of 1991, in Kobe and in Yokohama. I had made it happen, through the strength of an idea, perseverance, and the fearlessness to walk through a door and act like I belonged.

Why did we succeed? Was it just the idea? It was a fun idea, but surely other people had thought of something similar. By sheer luck, from the Japanese perspective we had solved the hardest part of the equation. We'd convinced a diverse group of ex-players, scattered across the US, to return to Japan for a modest sum and reconnect with their fans. From the perspective of Japanese sponsors and hosts of the event, I had solved the most unpredictable piece of the equation. By controlling that aspect, I created value and leverage. I had earned my spot at the table.

Like my first seed, in the travel space, my experience in representation and sports marketing was reasonably profitable but short lived. To a large degree, the biggest value I provided was access, particularly through language and communication. In the early 1990s, before the explosive growth of the internet, access was valuable. I was able to protect my position simply through my language and communication skills. As access turned into a commodity, it was harder to protect ideas. Nevertheless, I learned the power of ideas and a story. I believed they could get me through any door.

There are so many people who have ideas, but an idea is not worth the paper it's written on unless it's backed up by a plan. Every story I had also had a plan to back it up.

In Japanese, there is a homonym, 想像 (*sozo*, to imagine) and 創造 (*sozo*, to create or build). Many people have ideas. The ability to imagine and then to realize ideas is what separates the pretenders from the winners. I learned the value of ideas. But most importantly I learned the value of execution. Over time, I would find that the best way to protect an idea or a product is in its execution. In the ring, we talk about beating the opponent to the punch. In traditional Japanese martial arts, there is the concept of initiative (先), after-initiative (後の先) and pre-initiative, which comes before the other's initiative (先の先).

My third business was the result of meeting Robert Roche, who would become my second business brother. Our initial business venture together, H&R Consultants, helped support both of us through our early years in Japan. The real value came not from H&R, but from our continued partnership and friendship. I said earlier that my story is also Yumiko's story. My story is also Robert's story. The rest of this story would not have happened without meeting him. In all things, he inspired me to become a better businessman and person. I believe and hope that I have provided a similar value to him. Everything I subsequently achieved has a link to our meeting. Fate brought us together and I am eternally grateful.

In December 1990, my business career was off to a credible start. I was creating relationships and bridging people between the Chubu region and the US. I was young, confident, aggressive and wanted more. Yumiko and I were expecting our first child.

Meanwhile, US-Japan relations were at a low point. The trade deficit was constantly in the news. Japanese companies were buying Pebble Beach and Rockefeller Center. Nagoya and Chubu, the heart of the Japanese automobile and aerospace sectors, became a target. The US Ambassador to Japan had recently visited Chubu and in a fiery speech concluded that, "the Chubu region is the cause of the trade imbalance." If there was no Chubu, he reasoned, there would be no trade imbalance or tension between Japan and the US. There was tremendous pressure to solve this problem. In the field of aerospace, in particular, several joint ventures between major US and Japanese companies were quickly inked, and hundreds of American families were being relocated to Japan. This put Nagoya on the map.

Already in late 1990, there had been an influx of close to 50 American families as part of the new aerospace JVs. There was an expectation that another 150-200 families would be following them in the next 1-2 years. The US Consul General wanted to create a support organization for the incoming companies, like Boeing, McDonnell Douglas, Raytheon and Pratt Whitney, in the local community.

He organized the first meeting of the American Business Community of Nagoya, the ABCN, in December of 1990.

ENEMY OR FRIEND?

Robert and I met at this ABCN meeting. It was not love at first sight. We appeared to be reflections of each other — similar age, recently married, both just starting our respective businesses, Americans looking for the opportunities we thought Japan had to offer. At that first meeting it seemed we were confronted with a choice: compete or cooperate. Were we to be friends or enemies?

Nagoya seemingly wasn't big enough for both of us. That's the story we tell everyone. For the most part that was true. But, we clearly had some shared ideology and values. Those values are the basis of our ongoing friendship. One shared value is an adherence to the expanding cake theory. If there are more people at the table, it's time to bake a bigger cake. In each other, Robert and I saw the opportunity to get baking.

From the moment we met at the ABCN meeting, it was clear we had complementary skills. Robert was a trained lawyer and he already had built deep ties with the expatriate community. I had worked in the Japanese government, and my Japanese language skills and ties with the local business community at the time were stronger than Robert's.

We quickly recognized that our skills, experience and personalities were synergistic. The birth of the ABCN offered opportunity. Nagoya needed 'Japan-hands' — committed foreigners who immersed themselves in Japanese life — to successfully integrate a large influx of American families. We were uniquely qualified to service this need. We were in the right place at the right time. And we were better able to pursue this opportunity together than separately. And so, a partnership was born. A friendship was born. The results changed both of our lives for the better.

How was Nagoya going to cope with the influx of so many American families? Where were they going to live? How would they furnish their homes, buy cars, get driver's licences, figure out the lay of the land? Nagoya needed a reputable real estate and relocation services company for these major multinational corporations. There were a few small companies providing some of these services, but nothing sufficient to handle the coming wave. In Tokyo, there were several successful companies, like Ken Corporation, handling the expat market. Robert and I decided to create H&R Consultants, Nagoya's answer to Ken Corporation.

Karma and timing play an important role in my life. I believe in embracing opportunity. That's how I met my wife. That's how I took the call on the day I quit Yamaichi. Less than three months after our first meeting, Robert and I started showing apartments to the people of Boeing, McDonnell Douglas and Raytheon. We were in business.

Over the years, particularly in Chubu, Robert and I have often been mistaken for each other. Two sides of the same coin. But it is precisely because we were different and covered each other's backs, both professionally and personally, that our partnership and friendship has been so successful.

Appreciating and accepting the strengths and weaknesses of the other person is essential to any good relationship.

It's the key to any good business. Creativity springs from the dynamic differences of talented people. Later, when we worked together at OLM, and it was operating at its highest level, we often had lively, passionate disagreements. Everybody didn't necessarily like each other. But in the diversity and friction, we found strength and conviction. Like good sex, friction can be passionate and creative, as long as there is respect.

In the early 1990s, especially in Japanese, Robert came off as much rougher and more unreasonable than me. We'd go into a negotiation and he would lay out our position. He'd be blunt, aggressive and seemingly intractable. We'd meet resistance, and I would respond with a more polished and seemingly conciliatory position. But in effect, I had just said the same thing more eloquently. I seemed so much more reasonable. Our good cop, bad cop routine was very successful.

One final bit of karma. When my son, Ken, was born I became infected with chicken pox at the hospital. I was scheduled to give a speech to a local Japanese business group. As I was covered in lesions and running a high fever, I asked Robert to deliver the remarks in my stead. At that meeting, he met Tadashi Nakamura, which subsequently led to the birth of OLM, which is also a big part of this story. Again, karma.

ANOTHER WRONG TURN, THE REAL ESTATE YEARS

The Chairman was actually a tiny man, but his presence filled the room. With a shining bald head, broad shoulders, and a healthy tan gained from working outside, he exuded confidence, power and charisma. He had founded several businesses, including a construction company and a real estate management and development firm. He felt his mandate was to provide housing to humanity, or at least the people of Japan.

In Dave and Robert, I had found business brothers. Later in Nakamura, I had an older brother. In the Chairman, I felt I had found my business father and mentor. I learned more about business from him than from anyone else, but my success came after we parted ways, after I had slain him from my life (figuratively speaking, of course).

A business associate introduced me to the Chairman in the summer of 1990. The Chairman wanted to expand his business to the US, and he saw me as a conduit. Once again, my ability to communicate and bridge cultures was opening doors to opportunity. Japanese companies were flush with cheap money from Japanese banks and were buying properties across America. As noted, acquisitions of iconic properties like Pebble Beach and Rockefeller Center made the headlines. The Chairman was the king of his small empire. He aspired to more. He saw me as a means. I saw him as an opportunity. He took me under his wing.

Meeting Robert and deciding to join forces to provide relocation services to multinational corporations solidified my perceived worth to the Chairman. I suggested that he open up his existing high-end housing, and construct new luxury housing, to serve the growing American business community. He pounced on the idea. It served his desire to be international. It served his business interests. In fact, some of the first business we generated was in placing high-paying expatriates in luxury condominiums that the Chairman's company had built but had been unable to sell. We were able to re-package these white elephants as exclusive expatriate housing with rent that was 2-3 times greater than the general Nagoya market. A relationship was born.

Robert and I spent a lot of time with the Chairman. He gave us free space to use inside his office. We represented his companies and products to the expat community. We helped him set up a new 2x4 company, including the mechanism to import building materials from the US and Canada. In some ways, Robert and I competed for his attention, but I was the favorite son.

I would sit with him for hours individually and at the meetings of his board and executive team. At first I would only observe, but gradually I would participate too. He believed strongly in culture, vision and values. He was so passionate, so focused, and believed so strongly in the purpose of his companies that everybody around him believed, too. I believed. He taught me that great companies must have a strong sense of vision and purpose, a clear mission, values that matter, and a mandate to make the world a better place, all while making money. He had a loyal cadre of employees to whom he gave purpose and who did whatever he bid. I watched, I learned, I wanted to emulate him.

Of course, profit was paramount. But making money was always seen through the prism of delivering on our purpose. I saw first-hand that when people have a strong sense of purpose, they feel motivated because the job matters. When the job matters there's a strong sense of professionalism, because every task is meaningful. With purpose and professionalism, people feel empowered.

Ostensibly, the Chairman was the perfect mentor. A visionary leader, entrepreneur and businessman. However, there was a dark side. It took me too long to fully comprehend it or, to be more accurate, allow myself to believe it. I was so attracted to the facade and so overcome with the potential to make money that I believed the man's story rather than his actions.

A little after Robert and I had established H&R Consultants, the Chairman went to prison for tax evasion. He served almost two years. He was quite clear in explaining to me that the government was wrong. As he said, there is a law above the government. I later realized what he meant was that he was his own law.

During the time he was away, the luxury housing that we placed our clients in had problems, too. They were billed as top-of-the-line luxury condos, the best of the best. But little things failed quite often. The appearance was great, but the quality was suspect.

I also started to see problems in the operation's rank and file. The Chairman was charismatic and energetic. He would inspire his troops to give their all and to be their best. We worked long hours. We had a purpose and we all felt we were on the verge of even bigger payoffs. But the Chairman had a hair-trigger temper, often managing by temper tantrum. Somehow, when he would scream and yell, it would inspire us to work to make him happy. The president of the 2x4 company Robert and I helped the Chairman create died suddenly from overwork. An unfortunate casualty, who was quickly forgotten.

The Chairman was released from prison in 1995. Incarceration had not changed him. It had not diminished his spirit in any way. If anything, he was even more driven. Now his dream was to conquer the United States. And I was going to be his means to achieve that.

Through Dave, I had established many business contacts in the western parts of the United States, where the real estate market, particularly residential, was booming. A deal came to us for a master-planned community in a rapidly growing urban area; 2,000 homes, a golf course, a commercial town square, it was to literally be a small town, built from the ground up.

The Chairman had his beachhead to the US market. I was part of the advance team. There were promises to cut me into the deal. This was his chance to conquer America. His friends had tried, but as the economy came crashing down in Japan, many of his peers, who had invested in the US during the bubble years, were forced to retreat and tend their wounds. The Chairman knew he was smarter. He was mentoring me and I was to act as his proxy. This was my chance, too. Not only to get rich, but to make my name in my native country. Ego and greed can blind us. As I said earlier, what appears too good to be true almost always is.

From day one nothing went according to plan. Our partners in the project had worked magic with the city government to get the entitlements for the community approved, but the backroom dealing resulted in many of the city council members being voted out. The new council members had a different view of the project and the approval process came to a halt.

As the delays mounted, money ran out. It also was becoming increasingly clear that our partners were less than ethical.

The problems started mounting. We had to construct a main thoroughfare to be donated to the county. Each time we got close to being ready to pave, a weather event would essentially wash away the road and cause hundreds of thousands of dollars in damage. Different entities filed lawsuits against the project for lack of performance. Amid all the chaos, the two original partners, who had caused the mayhem, started fighting with each other. The Chairman and I flew back and forth on a monthly basis for two years. In Japan, I would spend 10 pm-to-midnight in meetings before going to sleep, then wake up at 6 am for hours of additional meetings.

The project had derailed. I offered to move to the US to take over the effort and attempt to salvage our dream. I had spent a couple of years serving as the apprentice and interpreter for the Chairman in our interactions with our partners. Their partnership had collapsed. We had to hire a new management team. The project was a runaway train. I needed to catch it, and at the same time learn how to drive it, or I'd get stuck on a speeding train.

The project itself started with the best intentions. It served a purpose. It also had the potential to make a tremendous amount of money. The purpose satisfied our ego. The profit potential blinded us to the ethical failings of our partners. Little things didn't add up, but greed kept us moving forward.

I learned an important lesson: good liars believe their own lies.

Sometimes it's not even so much a lie as an alternative reality. Our partners believed so implicitly in the value that they could create that they were positive the end would justify the means. Somehow or another, we would all make so much money that we could make any necessary adjustments later. If the project had actually gone according to schedule, that might have happened. Unfortunately, the reckoning never happened.

Commitments had been made not only to us as the investors, but to all the stakeholders in the project. Commitments that weren't being lived up to. Nothing was delivered on time. Nothing was delivered on budget. Everybody was fighting with the project. The original partners were fighting with each other. We were fighting with them. The Chairman went from temper tantrum to temper tantrum.

In December of 1997, I moved to the US with my family. I still believed in the project. We were building a town, a community. We were serving the greater good and there was plenty of money to be made. Or so I believed. But we were entangled in lawsuits with our partners; they had sued us, we had sued them. The city had sued the project, the project sued the city. And all of a sudden, I was running the project. I'm a fighter, but I was fighting multiple foes from all sides. This wasn't a fight, it was sheer chaos.

Prior to this time, I'd never been involved in a lawsuit. In many ways, I earned a psuedo law degree by fire. By far the most depressing moment was when our main bank sued us, including me individually, for the balance of the outstanding loan — more than $20 million. I felt like such a failure.

We often worked late hours. On my drive home one night, the road seemed darker, blacker than normal. I drove a grey Ford Expedition, a huge SUV that could power up our unfinished mountain so that we could explore all the potential land that was the basis of our dreams. I pulled into a parking area on Interstate 80. There were no other cars. When I turned off the engine, it was pitch black.

I sat just thinking in silence. My whole body was tense. My hands on the steering wheel were my only tether to the world.

1, 2, 3 …

Yumiko and I had four kids at this point, and I was thinking, "It's another lost day, another day that I didn't spend with my family."

If I had an accident now, with life insurance, I'd be worth more dead than alive. In retrospect, I understand that I wasn't really on the hook for the $20 million, but at the time the burden felt all mine. It was overwhelming. Every day was a slog, with no hope of getting better. "I'm never going to get out from under this," I thought. "It's hopeless."

I was down. I felt like giving up. I'd been hit from all sides and saw no way to win.

4,5,6 ...

I needed to re-find my purpose. Or, at this point, I needed to find the ability to move forward. Learning how to overcome and embrace failure is a skill.

Basketball superstar Michael Jordan once said, "I've missed more than 9,000 shots in my career. I've lost almost 300 games. Twenty-six times, I've been trusted to take the game-winning shot and missed. I've failed over and over and over again in my life. And that is why I succeed."

The very best hitters in baseball fail almost 70% of the time. We can learn from sports. The best of us fail, get up again and find a way to succeed. Sports can also be cautionary. Some people can't cope with failure. Boxer Mike Tyson and mixed martial arts star Ronda Rousey were never the same after losing. Once they lost their air of invincibility, instead of becoming stronger and better, they regressed. Rousey left the UFC completely.

In business, we all fail. But this time, my failure felt overwhelming. I was no longer a white knight. I was fighting with everybody. I was the face of this white elephant. I was the target of the Chairman's tantrums. I saw only downside. This was not my ticket to success, this was my downfall. When I succeed, it's because I can picture the outcome and find the means to achieve it. In later years, I realized that my true superpower is being able to inspire others and groups to envision and deliver. But on this night, in the total darkness of this highway rest area, I saw no way forward. I felt frozen and worthless.

7,8,9 ...

Finally, I roused myself to move. In those moments when there seem to be no good choices, the only choice is to move forward. The only option is to keep moving until you can see a way forward. In the absence of a compass, action always beats inaction.

Literally and figuratively, I couldn't see anything. The worst moments in my life have been when my senses shut down, when I could no longer see or hear or feel. Like at Morissa's funeral. This theme has repeated itself throughout my life. And on that darkest of nights, I was confronted with it again. But I had learned lessons, the hard way.

The first lesson I learned is that there's only one failure that can't be overcome or forgiven.

Death.

I'm not saying that all death is a failure. After all, it is the inescapable end-game in everybody's life. But any time one actually chooses death, and not to keep fighting, that's a failure. One that can't be forgiven. Because, if nothing else, you've chosen to forgo the option of finding a way to go forward.

The second lesson is that action creates opportunity. I function best when there's a plan, when I can envision the outcome. But not having a plan, or not yet having an idea of how to move forward, is not an excuse for not fighting. When I'm in the ring, sometimes I can't find a way to break my opponent's defense. If I don't throw punches and kicks, I will never find a potential opportunity to compete. The ideal, the goal, is to have a plan. In the absence of a plan, the only option is to fight. Again, I learned that on the playground.

The third thing is to have fun or do something else. There is always a choice.

Looking back, I wasted my time in those two years. It was difficult and I let that affect all my relationships.

My kids were wonderful, and Yumiko was always supportive. But in general, I was miserable. The worst thing that happened to me in that year and a half was that I got robbed of truly enjoying time with my children. And I'll never get that back. Ever. Children are only eight years old, or six, or five, or three, once. I've lost money and made it back. But time is something I can never recover. I waited too long to get up from the canvas and start fighting.

I pulled myself together and turned on the ignition of the car. I drove home. I walked into my silent, darkened house. I walked into the rooms of each of my children, Ken, Rian, Ellie and Mari. (Sean was not born yet.) They needed me, and I needed them. They gave my life purpose. I quietly got in bed with my wife. As always, she greeted me with a smile. To this day, whenever I come home, no matter what the hour, she greets me with a smile and says, "Thank you." Of course, I know my purpose. It is to be worthy of that gratitude, for her and my family.

So, we kept moving forward. We never completely fixed the development project, but we found a way through it. We were embroiled in a multitude of legal cases. We lost some, we settled some. I had inherited a losing proposition, but my team and I figured out a way. We had caught a speeding train and, in the end, we didn't crash and die.

I put a new team together. We took it out of bankruptcy. I was able to replace myself as the person in charge. We didn't turn a failure into a success, but we minimized the failure. That was probably the best that we could do. As a fighter, you need to learn from your losses. This was a loss, and I learned a lot from the experience.

BACK IN JAPAN, AGAIN

After just under two years, I returned to Japan in September of 1999. Yumiko and the kids had already repatriated in time for the Japanese school year in March. I hadn't abandoned Yumiko and my family during our time in the US, but I certainly hadn't been fully present either. America didn't offer the support structure Yumiko needed to raise our children, and my lack of time and presence exacerbated the problem. We agreed that we needed to return to Japan, where she was more comfortable and less dependent upon me. It took me another six months before I could fully rejoin them.

I stepped away from the day-to-day of the real estate project when I came back to Japan. There was a team in place. They were competent and knew what to do. After all the crazy problems, now it was just managing a real estate project. The project was moving slowly forward. It had not made the Chairman or me money. But from the outside, it now looked like an active, flourishing community. It looked like the project we had believed and invested in.

I was uncompensated for the effort, but out of a sense of responsibility I was still interfacing with the management team, starting and finishing my days on conference calls with the US. I no longer had the expectation of making my fortune with this entity. More than anything, I felt my responsibility was to ensure that the team I had assembled did not suffer from the whimsical wrath of the Chairman. And deep down, I still felt a responsibility to the Chairman, still inspired by his rhetoric and sense of purpose, and thankful for the lessons and opportunity he had given me.

As my involvement in the master-planned community was diminished, once again I needed to reboot. I had tried my hand in international exchange, travel, sports marketing and management, real estate development and relocation services, among other things. I had achieved success. I had been beaten up. I had experience as a one-man operation. I had built functioning teams. I'd worked with great friends and mentors, people who I still work with today. I had become involved with liars and cheats. I had fought battles, almost lost everything and fought back. I was not richer, but I had always found a way to support my family. We didn't have plenty, but I made sure that we always had enough. Rebooting didn't bother me, but I now craved something less opportunistic and more sustainable. Something that would satisfy my twin needs of purpose and profit.

I thought about joining H&R, the relocation company Robert and I had started, full time. But H&R had a president, and he was successful. That seemed like a step back rather than forward. I was the founder and co-chairman, and I thought that's where I should stay.

Once again, timing intervened. September 1999 was the height of the internet and IT bubble in Japan. It was relatively short-lived, but intense. An IT-focused company had recently partnered with OLM on a major sales project. They were particularly successful at selling digital services. They were notorious for their long, gruelling working hours, and their extremely successful sales force. Nobody would go home until the quotas were met. In April of 1999, they went public. In September, their share price had risen exponentially making their founder one of the richest men in the world. Less than two years later, the stock price would come crashing down, but the company is a survivor. They still do business today.

In September of 1999, however, they were at the height of their powers. They were impressed by how Robert and Nakamura used best practices from the US to build a best-in-class, sales-focused call center. They had a major investment in the launch of satellite television in Japan. Their goal was to apply their take-no-prisoners sales strategy to expanding satellite television. The partnership with OLM was to use a sales-focused call center to make outbound calls to sell satellite TV antennas. Their plan was to create a perfect ecosystem in which they had a stake in every piece of the business: the satellite television company; the sales company, Oak Lawn Marketing, and the installation company.

OLM at this time had been in business for about six years and was essentially three companies in one. There was a TV shopping division doing business as Shop Japan; a sourcing division for primarily US-origin products to be sold in Japanese retail; and a call center that answered the phone for Shop Japan, but also provided third-party services to other direct marketers, insurance companies and telephone companies. With the potential for exponential growth in conjunction with the launch of satellite television, Robert and Nakamura asked me to join OLM to run the call center divison. Our goal was to become the top sales-focused call center company in Japan and take OLM public in 6-12 months. Being tied in on the ground floor of the launch of the new satellite TV company was a massive opportunity.

Robert's pitch was simple: "Harry, we're going to make a massive amount of money, go public and make even more money." I agreed to join OLM to run the call center business, and my first major accomplishment solidified our partnership.

OLM had been growing and expanding so rapidly that its management and reporting systems still needed to catch up. We were good at selling. Our sales program with the satellite TV company was launched. We hired and trained our communicators. With our partner aggressively urging us on, we sold and sold. Every night at midnight, I would take a call from our partner to report on the number of units we had sold. The business arrangement was simple. We would make the sale. We would hand the work order to the installation company, who would contact the customer to install the satellite antenna. For every completed installation we would get paid at the close of the following month. Our partner assured us that the scheme was bulletproof. We made projections based on an assumption that 70% of our sales would be installed. We ran a worst-case scenario that showed our break-even point was at 30%.

For three months, our partner drove us hard. And we performed. We sold tens of thousands of units every month. We were killing it. We were building processes on the fly. After overseeing the complexities of building a master-planned community, this was a much easier process. The problem was that all the information flow was controlled by our partner. They demanded high performance from us, but offered very little information on how the installation company was progressing. We were selling and incurring costs relative to those sales, but we weren't getting paid.

As my team and I delved deeper, it turned out that less than 10% of our sales were actually being installed. Furthermore, the installation company didn't have the infrastructure to complete much more than they were actually doing. Our partner kept pushing us to do more, and faster, but the other side of the equation was unable to perform. Not only were we not getting paid, we weren't going to get paid. My first real valuable service to OLM was to call an emergency meeting with Robert and Nakamura to inform them that we were realizing profit on paper only, but would never actually collect. We stopped the business the day after this meeting.

I joined OLM to run the call center. As I was figuring out this business, I was still juggling several other endeavors, including the real estate project in the US, which I would visit every 6-8 weeks. I had several irons in the fire, but was increasingly looking for a single enterprise to fully focus on.

Over the years I've planted different types of seeds, and not all of them came to fruition. Some bloomed, like my early foray into cultural exchange and travel. It was a seed that bloomed but never recaptured its initial luster. The same with sports marketing. The real estate development effort was a seed that was planted and nurtured ... and never bloomed!

By 1999, I had a family of five children. I had achieved both success and failure, but I always made sure that I was able to take care of my family. We always had enough to eat. There was always enough money so that my children could try new things. We focused on experience, on skills and learning.

I made a deal with my kids. I would support them in any endeavor they wanted to try, but I had two conditions. They had to do their best. And they had to love it and have fun doing it. If they made that promise, Yumiko and I would find a way.

I also made a deal with Yumiko. I would always find a way to support us. She would make sure our home was in order. Both of our jobs, and our sense of responsibility, were absolutely essential for the success of our family. Yumiko was the rock, always providing positive energy. I am forever filled with admiration and thanks for that. Most importantly, she believed in me. No matter how difficult our situation, she never wavered in her belief or in expressing her gratitude. She taught me the power of true gratitude. Her gratitude inspired me to keep going even when I felt most defeated. Belief and gratitude provide inspiration. In later years, I used this value to get the most out of my staff. I say value, and not technique, because it must be sincere for it to have power.

I had planted many seeds along the way, but as yet had not created wealth. I was still hoping that the master-planned community project would make me money, but that was wishful thinking.

My pride drove me to stay involved. I thought it was a legacy project. Over time, I have seen time and again that the first movers in large real estate developments lay the groundwork and don't make the money. Often it is the second or even third operator who reaps the rewards. On paper, first-mover profit potential looks the greatest, but the first mover has to deal with significant entitlement and market timing risks. The second or third operator usually swoops in when the first level of entitlement, market timing and infrastructure risk have been significantly reduced.

My mentor, the Chairman, had taught me these lessons. He had made his money in Japan primarily by being the second or third mover. In the US, we had violated his own rules for doing business. Big opportunity, big dreams, but big risk. My pride and my lingering respect for the Chairman kept me involved in the project. I wanted him to succeed. His lessons meant something to me.

And I also still wanted to believe that I could make a windfall for myself, that all my time and effort had not been wasted.

"I COULD HAVE YOU KILLED"

By 2002, the constant juggling was becoming less and less sustainable. I had too little time in the day to spend on OLM, the real estate project, my other projects and, most importantly, my family. I was spread too thin.

Around that time, I set a rule for myself. Often, I would wake up around 5 am, and toss and turn for a while, before falling back to sleep for another hour or so. I realized that I never felt significantly more rested when I awoke after going back to sleep. And so, I vowed that as soon as my eyes opened, I would get out of bed to start my day. I still abide by that. This has lengthened my day, and I found that my most productive hours were in the morning before my family woke up. I was able to translate those hours into work, and the hours gained working into spending time with my family. This proved to be much more valuable to me than being half asleep.

It was late February of 2002. I had just gotten off the plane from another whirlwind, uncompensated trip to check up on the master-planned community in the western part of the United States. With the Chairman, business always came first, so from the airport I went straight to his house to report to him and his CFO on the state of the project. The flight arrived at around 4 pm, so I probably got to his house a little after 5.00 with my bags in tow.

The news from the project was getting steadily better. It had stabilized. It was cash flow positive. There appeared to be a path to recoup some or potentially all of the investment. Profit, especially after factoring in the cost of money, seemed unlikely. The potential for me to make anything diminished with each passing day. I was performing an unpaid service out of a sense of duty.

The Chairman's house is a testament to his ego. Most of this colossal structure is a showroom of his success and wealth where he holds court for people to plead their case for his business and interest. For years this was my standard, my goal. But I had spent hours in his house. Hours in the living area in front of his kitchen, waiting to be summoned. In this huge home, he spent the most time and conducted most of his business in his kitchen. His wife and his children had much smaller, humble living quarters hidden above this grandiose testament to his business acumen. I had gotten to know his two sons, who ultimately turned their backs on him. I was more his son than they were. This was the abode of his family, but it was not a home.

I sat in the waiting area with his CFO. I pre-briefed him on the status of the project, and we waited. The Chairman had purchased a new Rottweiler puppy and it had just been delivered. He was overjoyed. He decided to invite the dog breeder to have dinner with him at his kitchen table. His wife served. The CFO and I waited. The hours on the clock ticked from 6 to 7 to 8. I had been waiting in the sitting room for more than three hours. It was dark in the room because nobody had turned on the light. I could occasionally hear him roughhousing with the dog.

I was waiting to give him a report that I had already given to his CFO. I was tired. I was grimy from close to 20 hours of traveling. I was sitting in this monstrosity of a house, which was presumed to be a testament to the vision and purpose this man so eloquently espoused, but was really only a monument to his ego and greed. Nobody in this place was happy, except for one man.

Finally, after close to four hours of waiting, I was summoned. I actually had some pretty good news on the project, but of course, we returned to the same old themes. Once again, we rehashed the history. At some point during that conversation, when we were going through the issues, and reliving years of miscues, he stopped. He was enraged. Enraged that for all his screaming, tantrums and bullying, the project was not going to be a monument to his genius. He had not conquered America. He eyed me dispassionately. "Harry, for the money I've invested in this project, I could have you killed. You know that, don't you?"

I was stunned. My mentor, my father figure, was threatening to have me killed.

Stunning, but liberating. I owed this man nothing. He had built an empire on the backs of people like me. I had come to like and respect these comrades. I had fought with them and broken bread with them. And all of them were still chasing the pot of gold. I had seen people around him work themselves to death and have nervous breakdowns. I had watched his family run and hide from him. I had been driven by a belief in his powerful words, a belief in the purpose. But mostly I had been driven by greed disguised in the cloak of purpose.

Now the facade had tumbled down.

I had been the victim of the sunken cost fallacy. I had deceived myself into thinking I had sunk too much time and energy into this debacle to walk away. I'm sure that the

Chairman implicitly understood this. When people were fully bought in, I had watched him do with them whatever he chose, with no thought of consequences or repercussions. He would get everyone around him all-in, and then raise the stakes so that only he could play and only he could win. I realized that I had allowed him to do that to me.

I looked at him with new clarity. But more importantly, I re-evaluated my position. No matter how hard I worked, no matter what positive outcome I might deliver, it was never going to be my success. I was being driven by a sense of responsibility, but I realized, "I owe this man nothing."

I stood up. "Thank you. I appreciate the fact that we've done business for this long, but we are now done."

That was it. I left. The CFO followed me out. He knew I was angry, but he had seen these scenes before. They all expected me to come back. I never did.

I was still the representative director of their US entities. I formally resigned from everything within hours of walking out.

I explained everything to the team in the US. They were not shocked. I'm still friends and do business with some of them. They understood. The CFO, another comrade, tried to convince me to come back. I told him to stop calling. He did.

I've never seen or talked to the Chairman again. Our split was one of the best decisions I've ever made. I had bigger and better things to do. The first big step to the next level of success was walking away with no regrets and no strings attached. He had been my mentor. Many of the lessons I'd learned were negative, but I was ready to constructively apply those hard-won lessons. I had been through the wringer, been battered about, and was a finely honed fighting machine. I now needed to find the right focus for my talents. I needed to find the right fight.

GOOD TO GREAT

H&R Consultants had been folded into OLM and I had cut all ties with the US real estate project. I made the decision to focus all my energy into OLM.

Organizationally, OLM was facing the same crisis of focus that I was.

When I had started working with them in 1999, it was three disparate operating entities: a TV shopping division, a product-sourcing-for-retail sales division, and the call center division. Each of those divisions was treated like a separate business, and none of them were excelling. In 1999, with the satellite TV deal in hand, it appeared that the greatest opportunity was in the growth and running of call centers. When that deal imploded, the call center was just another business to keep going.

Robert, Nakamura and I, along with a few other members of upper management, spent countless hours debating the strategy and future of the company. We got together every Saturday for a planning session. We encouraged each other to study. We were constantly learning and seeing how we could improve. Some of the books that influenced us included Jack Stack's *The Great Game of Business*, Spencer Johnson's *Who Moved My Cheese*, and Stephen R. Covey's *The Seven Habits of Highly Effective People*. The book that ended up having the greatest influence on us as a group was *Good to Great*, by Jim Collins. It described the thought process of companies that became high performing for a sustained period of time. We decided to adopt the tenets of the book.

Part of that process was to define our 'hedgehog concept,' the one thing that: 1) We loved to do; 2) Would make us money; 3) We could become the best in the world at. We decided that our path was to be the world's best TV shopping infomercial company. We identified power branding, which we subsequently renamed Shop Jabranding, as the flywheel that drove our business.

Just like that, OLM's years as a juggling act were over. We no longer spread our resources and our talent across three disparate businesses. We became laser focused. We had a core business model. We'd clearly defined what we did and how we did it. Robert and Nakamura were the two strong leaders of OLM. Robert's strength is in finding new opportunities. He is the best and most talented person I've ever known at building new businesses from scratch. Nakamura's strength is in building relationships. His tireless focus on building a network with the Japanese TV stations allowed OLM to gain traction. At the time, we were one of about ten infomercial companies in Japan. Our first order of business was to separate ourselves from the field. We needed to go from one of many to number one. And we needed to do it quickly.

Around this time, Robert was consulting with his brother and confidant, Ed. Ed asked him, "Who do you think is the best person other than yourself at Oak Lawn Marketing?" Robert replied, "Harry." So, Ed asked, "Where's the biggest opportunity?" "Shop Japan." "Where's Harry?" "He's running the call center." Robert shared this conversation with Nakamura and me. This happened around February of 2002, precisely when I had decided to stop juggling and focus exclusively on OLM. I was put in charge of Shop Japan.

A sharpening of strategic focus changed the vector for the company, and for each of us on the management team. We stopped thinking about all the different types of business we could potentially succeed at. We focused solely on realizing the full potential of Shop Japan. We were still Oak Lawn Marketing, but our intent was now to become the best and biggest infomercial company in Japan. And I was in charge of that business.

The summer after taking over as the director of Shop Japan, I took a management training course at my alma mater, Cornell. I started the process of defining my leadership principles.

I wanted to codify my hard-won lessons. My experience with my mentor, the Chairman, bothered me. He spoke of vision, mission and values. He espoused purpose. He was charismatic and in a business that was meaningful. He exuded credibility. I had believed in him. He had hundreds of people in his organization who believed in him. He provided them with a sense of purpose. They would do anything for him.

Reluctantly — and I say reluctantly because I genuinely wanted to believe in all that — I came to the realization that for all the high-mindedness, he was really only driven by personal greed.

He was exceptional at setting what appeared to be achievable hurdles for incentives. Yet no one ever achieved these milestones. And the hurdles kept rising as soon as anyone appeared to be on the verge of surmounting them. He was the master at getting people to work harder, by providing purpose and the potential for personal reward. But his actions, rather than his words, made it clear that profit was more important than keeping his customers or his employees happy. And the profits needed to come to him first, and ultimately stay with him.

The Chairman was my mentor. I learned the importance of culture, of having a clear vision, mission and values. I wanted to be part of an organization that didn't just espouse purpose, but actually delivered on its vision while generating profit. Robert, Nakamura and I all came to desire this same goal. We had created the Shop Jabranding flywheel, a powerful way to do business, but we needed to fully develop the culture. We needed to find a strong purpose. As I rose in leadership and responsibility at OLM, I took the lead in building the culture.

MY LEADERSHIP PRINCIPLES: VICES

I created an acronym, VICES, to describe my leadership philosophy. It stands for Vision, Integrity, Competency, Efficiency and Sustained Success. I think every great leader in some manner touches on these areas.

The acronym is a description, proscription and warning. It is a warning to leaders, including myself, to avoid believing so implicitly in ourselves that we lose sight of right or wrong. To not become so addicted to our power to lead that we focus only on our personal benefit, rather than to serve a purpose.

Vision provides a shared sense of purpose. If we believe in the purpose of our organization, team or group, we feel both motivated and responsible. Providing purpose means that each person and every action contributes to a meaningful outcome. It builds a sense of pride and professionalism because all activities contribute to our vision. This is exactly what I felt was missing when I worked on Wall Street. Purpose makes every action meaningful. It is deliberate. Purpose — a clearcut 'why' — must guide not only the whole of the organization, but every project or team within it.

At our peak in OLM, we would challenge each other on actions small and large with the question 'Why?' If we couldn't find a sense of purpose, we wouldn't take the action.

Integrity is about trusting. Many people say, "You have to earn my trust." That's bullshit. The best way to build trust is to give trust, to provide an environment based on trust and integrity. As a leader, I will take the critical first step. I will trust first. That doesn't mean that I don't check. Of course, there is accountability. And real trust comes from accountability. I gave you a job and you performed. We can build from there. But when I trust someone, truly trust them, I can see their level of commitment to me and the company go up.

At Shop Japan, we built on that sense of trust. Not only did we trust each other, we trusted our customers. Our unconditional 39-day money-back guarantee was premised on trust and gratitude. Our customers were purchasing our product without physically inspecting it. We gave them the opportunity to use the product for 39 days to ensure that it met their expectations. If not, they returned it and we refunded their money.

One New Year's season, my staff was faced with a dilemma. We were selling fresh crab from Hokkaido, a perishable food product. They showed me our TV infomercial. It didn't include our unconditional money-back guarantee. I asked why not. The reply was that the product was food. It was perishable. We couldn't take it back. I asked my staff whether we believed in the product. They replied, "We do!" We changed the offer to, "Buy today, and if you don't think it is delicious, call us and we will refund your money." We had actually tested a show without the money-back guarantee. The episode with the guarantee performed 20% better. Nobody called requesting a refund.

We trusted our customer. We made more money. Trust and integrity are not a cost. They create a virtuous circle.

For me, integrity was also about transparency. We instituted open-book management at OLM. Everybody in the organization knew how the company was performing, knew what was delivering profit and what wasn't. We were a team. All of our bonuses were linked to the profitability of the business as a whole, and secondarily to individual performance. The hurdles didn't change. The incentives were clear. There were no false promises of riches that would never materialize. Integrity is about trust, accountability and transparency.

We took it a step further. In our new offices, we made our walls glass and instituted an open-door policy. While we did have blinds for the occasions that absolutely demanded privacy, in general everyone in the office could see what other people were doing. Everybody would see me throughout the work day. I was accountable too.

Competency, for a leader, is more than being knowledgeable or skilled. For the purpose-driven team, every task is meaningful, so every task requires a sense of professionalism. Too often, leaders focus only on the star individuals or the biggest drivers of performance. Stars come and go and the drivers change with time. I realized that a true leader must show interest and appreciation at every layer of our organization, for every job and task. When every job has purpose, not only do groups function better, but everyone in every task takes greater pride in their work and knows they will be acknowledged.

Competency is about building systems and processes that drive decision-making. At OLM and Shop Japan, we built codified ways to evaluate new products and measure all the drivers of our business. Intuition, creativity and experience (as well as luck) were essential to our success, but only after our processes and systems helped us quantify the opportunity. Perfecting our way of doing business allowed us to make average talent good, good talent great, and great talent exceptional.

I think the current concerns about artificial intelligence (AI) replacing jobs and people are misguided. I'm a firm believer in AI supplementing people, so we can do our jobs better and focus our actions on what only human beings can do. In my current role, as owner of a health and fitness business in Japan, we use technology so we can provide better service and hospitality to our members. Better systems and processes allow us to provide greater personalization and friendliness.

A good leader creates both expertise and redundancy in our organizations. If we've created good systems and processes, nobody is indispensable. While I always wanted to find and retain exceptional talent, I would emphasize to everyone that I wanted us, as a team, to be better because you or I are here, but never dependent on us.

When I first became CEO, I would occasionally participate in management meetings where someone would blurt out, "This person is so important to us that we can't afford to lose them." My reply was always the same: "If that is true, let's fire them tomorrow. Let's learn how to survive without them right away because we must never allow ourselves to be dependent on any single source of failure. And that even applies to me." Competency is about making people better, not about dependency.

Different layers of our organizations have greater or lesser degrees of responsibility. Yet, as leaders, we must value and respect each and every part. We must professionalize every process to maximize performance and motivation. We have to establish a culture that says the way we do things matters, and instills pride. If we take that away, if we make our followers think they're merely a cog in the machine, we take away their connection to the purpose. If we fail to value competency, the motivation of our groups will rot from within. Competency matters, and must be recognized and valued.

In Japan, there is a concept of *Do*, the way. Appreciating and understanding competency creates a way for everyone. Just like *Budo*, the way of the warrior, or *Chado*, the way of tea, we had Shop Japan-do, the way of Shop Japan. Great leaders and great teams create their own way.

Efficiency is particularly important for leaders to focus on because it's so easy for people to overwork when driven by a strong purpose. In Japan, where I live and work, this is particularly true.

I don't really believe in work-life balance. I think it's a fiction. That's not how the world works. There should be work-life harmony, but sometimes we need to work a 60-hour-plus week. At times, that's the most effective choice. As leaders, cultivating an environment that allows our team to focus when they need to focus, and recharge when they need to recharge, creates an environment for success.

When I've seen greatness in others and myself, it usually comes from concerted effort. Leaders don't just allow for these spurts, they demand them. So, great leaders must also ensure a time for rest and rejuvenation.

I am a firm believer in stress. Growth and learning come from stress. A simple analogy is weight training. Stressing the muscles causes regeneration, growth and strength. Failing to balance the stress with rest and recuperation causes injury and failure. The book *Range: How Generalists Triumph in a Specialized World*, by David Epstein, explains the science of stress as it relates to both learning and sports. I was incorporating these principles of stress in my leadership even before I understood the science behind them. The most efficient way to achieve high performance is to balance stress with time off. Not work-life balance, but a routine more conducive to high performance: stress and rest.

There is another reason why work-life harmony is important to me. As a leader, we are models for our followers, for the community and for society. I feel a responsibility to treat our team how I hope other business leaders treat their employees. If employees are not treated and compensated fairly, who will be the customers for our products and services?

Sustained Success. It sounds so simple. Of course, we need sustained success. As leaders it is essential to create an environment that celebrates little wins as well as set big, bodacious goals. There's nothing wrong with big goals, but it's important to set meaningful milestones, both to check current course and speed, and to ensure everyone stays sharp. We need to have little wins along the way because big goals can take a long time to tackle.

My own experience taught me the dangers of inertia. Inaction and inertia are often more damaging than little losses. In fact, healthy organizations allow for a balance of little wins against little losses. Little losses are learning opportunities. Big losses are a big problem.

As OLM got bigger, I saw an increasing fear of failure. This sort of anxiety causes inertia, and inertia costs as much, and sometimes more, money than failure. If we fail, we can learn and move forward. If we stand still, it gets harder and harder to restart. The bigger the ship, the harder it becomes to change course.

When I practice fighting, probing the opponent is just as important as trying to load up for a knockout. I know that in the course of a round I will inevitably be hit. My focus is to not sustain damage, more than not to be hit. If the opponent is competent, they will score. That's OK. I need to score more. Sometimes I might get a knockout, but if I score more than my opponent, I win. In the course of a round or a fight, there are multiple times to win little victories and take little losses. Staying focused on the purpose while creating little wins is important in the process of progressing toward the big win.

People who don't know how to embrace and learn from failure scare me. When 1 interview mid-level people or higher, 1 always ask, "Tell me about a failure and what you learned from it."

Sometimes they reply, "I've never had a major failure." 1 run away from any supposedly experienced middle-aged people who give that reply. 1 also run away from the person who lays all the blame on other people. "Yes, 1 failed," I'll hear, "but it was all because of so and so." They don't hold themselves accountable. Accountability starts with individual responsibility. Successful people search for personal responsibility. They examine the circumstances, and ask of themselves and their team what they could have done better. In organizations we almost never fail alone. But the most valuable people, especially managers, are the ones who take failure personally, and look for what they could have done better, rather than focus on why their team members suck.

We will all face failure in our lives. How we overcome it is the mark of character and grit. If a potential employee is unable to share a story of character or grit, or truly hasn't experienced it yet, they are too risky to employ. 1 don't want their first experience with adversity to be on our dime.

1 don't hold younger recruits to the same standards. But even with younger people, 1 find that those who've been active in team sports have a healthier attitude about losing and learning from mistakes. Younger people will make mistakes, and that educational cost is part of our responsibility at the company. 1 hold mid-career hires to a higher standard. 1 expect them to have graduated from entry-level mistakes.

One of my best qualities is the fact that I've had some pretty big failures, and have come back stronger. When 1 look at the people I surround myself with, I feel most comfortable working with those who I know have been knocked down, and got back up. I want those people on my team when rough times inevitably come. At OLM, we literally created a battalion of battle-tested employees. We were exceptional when our backs were against the wall.

The VICES acronym is meaningful to me. Occasionally people challenge me about the 'C.' What about charisma?

As leaders, we need charisma. I have been told on numerous occasions that I've got 'rizz.' I've come to believe that effective leadership charisma is the sum of my VICES principles, combined with passion. Passion and VICES create an aura of charisma. Yet, I have known many people with charisma who lack an appreciation of these leadership principles, and are without a moral compass. These leaders are dangerous, because they enlist followers only to sacrifice them for their personal gain.

Hence, the warning embedded in the acronym. A great leader creates a sense of purpose and belonging. A great leader creates truth for their organization. A great leader is passionate and charismatic. But yes, there is a fine line between passion and addiction. Almost every successful leader I know walks this fine line. As a leader, when we feel like we are creating our own truth or our own reality, it's easy to succumb to the dangers of power, alcohol or drug abuse, sexual obsession, or all of these vices at once. Uncontrolled passion is lust, which is a powerful addiction. Controlled passion leads to success. It is my last essential characteristic of a great leader.

I had formed a clear vision of the leader, the manager and the follower I wanted to be, and of the types of employees I wanted to stand with me. I had built on the lessons of my mentor and I was resolved not to fall victim to excess and greed. I had my roadmap for leadership. I was ready, and wanted to assume the helm at OLM.

BECOMING NUMBER ONE

OAK LAWN MARKETING REBOOT

At OLM, we made a conscious decision to reboot. Our first goal was to become the number-one infomercial company in Japan. To get there, we focused on three key initiatives. First, to differentiate ourselves from our peers. Second, to better understand and appreciate our customer. And third, to find the right talent to grow our team.

Following the principles of *Good to Great*, we had defined the Shop Jabranding process as our means to be better than our peers. As mentioned, at that time we were one of about ten companies doing what we did. Often, we were all trying to sell the same things, as US suppliers mass-distributed products to all of us rather than granting exclusive distribution rights to any one company.

Part of our business model relied on finding the most successful infomercial products from around the world to sell in Japan. We and several other companies had established that there was an untapped market for these global hit products, but without exclusive distribution rights for Japan, we often cannibalized each other.

Our first order of business was to establish a better sourcing and contracting protocol than our peers. Robert had been quite close with a company from Canada that was one of the TV shopping innovators. We joined forces with them, as well as with a similar company doing business in the UK and Germany, to form a Global Alliance (GA) to negotiate with suppliers. Each of us individually struggled to secure exclusive distribution rights for our respective territories, but by combining our buying power we provided a one-stop shop for a company with a hit product in the US to immediately gain access to four international territories.

At the beginning of the GA, several suppliers also complained to us that OLM had a reputation as being difficult to work with — slow to respond and arbitrary in how we accepted or rejected products. Starting in February of 2002, when I took responsibility for Shop Japan, Robert and I committed to changing this image. We bound ourselves to performance metrics for both speed to market and minimum annual sales goals. We made a choice to create a reputation as the most responsive and performance-focused company in our field.

The GA, and establishing clear performance metrics, quickly enabled us to change the perception of OLM in the industry. To put the transformation in perspective, in the first year of the GA we purchased about US $10 million of products. By the fifth year, we were purchasing 10 times that amount.

Of course, our business was about selling, not purchasing. With exclusive distribution rights, however, we sold more products, more profitably. Suppliers took note. Now they wanted us to have exclusive rights to their products. They wanted to be part of our machine. Instead of playing us off against our competitors, we became the first choice of companies that had a verified direct-response TV (DRTV) hit product.

The first step in our ascent to number one was to improve our supply chain process. We accomplished that quickly, efficiently and tremendously effectively. We left our competition behind.

PEOPLE ARE PEOPLE

The second initiative was to focus more deeply on our customer. We had espoused the belief that people are people, but in fact we hadn't fully embraced this value.

When searching for a product from overseas, best-selling items had been presented to our team but, after often long deliberation, they'd be rejected on the vague premise that 'it wasn't right for Japan.' The reason was always some variation on the theme of Japanese exceptionalism, which was especially prevalent in the heady years of the economic bubble. "The Japanese colon is different." "Japanese snow is different." And so on. This was a factor contributing to our reputation as being slow and arbitrary.

Robert and Nakamura had already debunked several myths in the building of OLM. In the early- and mid-90s Japanese TV stations still went dark during the midnight hours. Prior to the advent of the infomercial, US stations also went off the air. Infomercial companies taught the market that it was possible to monetize the overnight hours on TV. Initially, Japanese stations refused to sell their midnight slots to OLM because "nobody watches at that time."

Of course, if nothing is aired, that becomes a self-fulfilling prophecy. We were one of the first to convince TV stations to let us try to monetize that time. Other companies quickly followed suit, and the media companies realized there was an underserved market in those hours, not only for advertising but for programming.

OLM was also one of the first companies in Japan to offer 24-hour order-taking service at our call center. When we finally started airing during the overnight hours, we had to convince buyers that they could call between the hours of 9 pm and 5 am. When Robert and Nakamura asked our outsourcing partner to provide 24-hour service, they demurred. "Japanese consumers are perfectly happy to call during normal daytime hours," they were told. We had to build our call center, which I ran for the first few years of my career at OLM, in order to offer round-the-clock service. The order volume on our midnight airings doubled or tripled. Once again, the market quickly followed our lead.

OLM had already proved many times over that challenging the notion of Japanese exceptionalism could lead to a blue ocean of opportunity. With products, however, we still clung to the belief that we needed to determine if the item, regardless of how big a hit it was overseas, was right for Japan, because the Japanese consumer was 'different.'

General Electric CEO Jack Welch famously said, "Think global, act local." Of course, Japan is unique, but in its culture, not in individuals' needs and desires. Robert and I had made the decision to be committed Japan-hands — to invest in understanding Japan so that we could find innovative business opportunities, particularly with US products and services trying to gain access to the country. We had learned how to communicate with the Japanese, and marketing is communication. It was not a matter of the Japanese consumer having unique needs that were fundamentally different from the US or European consumer. It was a matter of how best to understand and communicate the fulfilment of those needs.

Not only was there a myth of Japanese exceptionalism, but there was also the myth of monolithism. By that time, both Robert and I had both spent more than 15 years in Japan. We knew that the Japanese people were not an undifferentiated mass, immovably set in its ways. But we would be in meetings, both external and internal, where we would be 'Japan-splained' to – knowingly advised that, "We Japanese don't watch TV during the midnight hours. We Japanese are happy to call during regular hours." Even though we had contributed to busting these myths, we too could become prey to groupthink.

One of our international partners in the GA called bullshit on this. Wanting to have a cleaner home; wanting to sleep better; wanting to look and feel better; wanting to eat better – these are universal human needs and desires, not unique to any country or people. They know no borders.

Our business was to look for problems or complexes that people have in their daily lives and present a solution. Long-form DRTV presents to the customer demonstrable solutions for everyday problems. How to look, sleep, feel, clean and cook better.

Instead of letting our customers tell us their needs, we'd been acting as the exclusionary gatekeeper to best-selling products from around the world. We erroneously assumed that we were smarter than our customers.

We eventually came to our senses and decided to put the customer first.

We took down the defenses. If a product was a verified hit, we stepped out of the way. We made it our mantra to let the Japanese consumer decide. We would research all the reasons why a product or service had become a smash hit in the US, Canada or Europe. It was not up to us to decide what hit products from around the world the Japanese consumer wanted. They could tell us themselves, via the power of their pocketbook.

This sounds so simple, but it required a monumental change in our mindset. When we looked at a hot product from another country, instead of trying to judge if it was right for Japan, we instead focused on understanding what was in its DNA that made it successful, and how to best communicate those attributes.

This change of perspective effectively separated us from our competitors. It allowed us to focus on speed to market. The results were quick and undeniable. One of our great internal stories is when Nakamura first saw a product called the Steam Buggy, a portable steam-cleaning device that was a major hit in the US and Europe. "There is no way this yellow monstrosity will work," he argued. "If it does, I'll shave my head." The Steam Buggy became our first mega-hit, using our new customer-driven criteria, and Nakamura's head stayed shaved for the next several years.

At the first trade show I attended immediately after taking over Shop Japan, I used our new approach to secure the rights for two products. One was Bun & Thigh Max and the other was True Sleeper.

Initially, the representative for the two products didn't want to take a meeting with us. As I mentioned before, we had a poor reputation. I explained that I was the new guy running the show, and that we had a new, more aggressive approach to testing and launching products. Robert and I cajoled her and her colleagues for two days. They finally acquiesced. Two months later, we aired an infomercial for Bun & Thigh Max, a resistance exercise device that turned into one of our first successful fitness products. Two months after that we aired True Sleeper, which Shop

Japan still sells today. This memory foam mattress topper is far and away OLM's longest- and best-selling brand, with cumulative sales in excess of US $1.5 billion.

Without True Sleeper, there might not have been a continuation of this story. Our first two initiatives worked hand in hand to quickly change the trajectory of the company. The last initiative was to ensure that we had full buy-in from our staff in our direction. We had to make sure we had 'the right people on the bus.'

BATTLE SCARS

Our third major challenge was to find and retain excellent staff. When I became CEO in 2006, we were a hungry and scrappy company. We were headquartered in the manufacturing and shipping hub of Nagoya. This was Toyota country. We wanted to hire the best and the brightest. We tried to copy the hiring methodology of the Toyotas of the world. We even hired a human resources director from Nissan.

For the elite workforce, however, there were more appealing options than Oak Lawn Marketing. For the most part, nobody knew who we were. We were in an industry, direct marketing and TV shopping, that was considered non-traditional and therefore untrustworthy. The company was run by a bunch of foreigners. Even our name, when pronounced in Japanese, sounded unappealing. The 'lawn' of Oak Lawn sounded like 'loan.' Loan companies in Japan have a dubious reputation.

By necessity, we had to adopt an innovative approach to identifying and hiring talent. One of our first decisions was to become the company for second chances. Japan is notoriously unforgiving of failure. We offered those who possessed the right skills and motivation, but may have stumbled in the past, a second chance.

As I outlined earlier, we hired talent who had failed and boldly owned it. OLM mid-career hires were looking for a new opportunity for a reason. That didn't scare us if the individual appeared to have learned from prior mistakes.

Our first important hires were for the most part battle-scarred and appreciative of a second chance. They were the core members of the new Shop Japan and Oak Lawn Marketing. I was always interested in their journey and admired and valued their experience, including failure. Sooner or later, we all confront failure.

We had a team of seasoned, bruised and battered veterans who were loyal to both the company and to me. I could trust them to watch my back at all times. And they knew I had their back. We had a deep trust in each other, which was one of the reasons we were able to build our culture and change our business practices so thoroughly and successfully in a remarkably short time.

We embraced diversity. We gave women equal opportunity. There was no wage gap. We provided as much support and opportunity as possible for women with children. We hired non-Japanese. We offered flex time work scheduling. We became a leading company in our approach to diversity. Later, in 2015, I was recognized by the Japanese Cabinet as a male leader of change. Of course, I believed in our progressive workplace culture. In truth, however, we developed our culture because without it we couldn't compete with the Toyotas of the world for talent. We needed to find another way.

From the perspective of traditional Japanese companies, we were outsiders. I was invited to a small business meeting between the Chubu chapter of the American Chamber of Commerce in Japan and leaders of the Chubu Economic Federation. At one point in the discussion about education abroad, the president of one of the major corporations stated emphatically that he thought a year of study abroad was beneficial, but anyone who had graduated from a university outside of Japan was too tainted by foreign culture to be trusted. This closed way of thinking in traditional Japanese industry was in fact an opportunity for us. We embraced second chances, women returning to the workforce, and Japanese who had worked, studied or graduated abroad. Instead of trying to be the same, we accepted being different.

As our talent pool within the company became more diverse, we focused on creating a unique and powerful culture. We were entrepreneurial, but were preparing to be more than Robert's or Nakamura's or Harry's company.

By becoming a company of opportunity for anyone with talent and passion, regardless of circumstances, once again we changed our vector. In Japan, the new company year starts in April, so it's typical for graduating students to start on 1 April. The first year that we opened the door for new graduates to apply, we only had only a handful of submissions. By 2016, we had more than 2,000 applicants and our full-time workforce exceeded 500. We went from being a company nobody had heard of in a fringe industry to a model employer that people were lining up to work for. The decisions we made mattered, and they generated long-term results.

We didn't make these decisions solely based on our moral compass. We found the most effective way to hire and retain good people to ensure our long-term survival. Trying to copy Toyota didn't work. We took a different lesson from Toyota — the carmaker's concept of *kaizen*, or continuous improvement. We were relentless in the pursuit of best practices, particularly for the direct marketing industry. We were constantly learning and sharing effective methodologies with others in the industry, driven by the recognition that today's best practice will be tomorrow's normal operating procedure, and soon may be obsolete.

As we became a leading company, we found that others started to copy us. If we did a 30-day money-back guarantee, or an offer like: "Taste it, and if you don't like it we'll give you your money back," our competitors followed suit. Since many would copy our offers, we placed an even greater emphasis on best-in-class operations. We wanted our model behavior to set us apart.

Prior to 2003 or 2004, most companies dubbed US home-shopping show audio into Japanese and aired an episode until the product stopped selling. The life cycle for a product was usually around 12-18 months. Very little investment or time went into improving the shows or the products, because by the time any changes were made, the life cycle had expired.

In our journey to become number one, we made a concerted effort to extend the life cycle of the products. We pivoted to using Japanese customer testimonials as our voice. We used our call center to find the best Japanese advocates of our products and featured them. Real people, telling real stories. We made our customers the star of our shows. It was a form of reality TV and we did it better than anyone else in Japan.

We became exceptional at creating Japan-based content with Japanese consumers. We became proficient at creating super shows that combined the best and most compelling content from the US programming with our locally created content. The synergistic shows were significantly more effective than either a purely US production or a purely Japanese one. We blended the best of the two cultures together.

Our conversations and interactions with our customers kept getting deeper. This allowed us to make improvements in quality and service. We started modifying our shows based on the customer voice. Prior to launching True Sleeper, we churned through products continuously. Starting with True Sleeper, we started to create long-selling products and brands. The better and deeper the conversation we had with our customers, the longer the life cycle of our offerings, which also drove up our revenue and profit. This was our value- and profit-driving model.

As our approach and expertise evolved, our suppliers now looked at us as more than mere distributors of products. We truly became their marketing partners.

In 2002, we had made a decision to change our approach. We focused on being the best TV shopping company in Japan. We hired a team and nurtured a culture. We defined our way of doing business. By 2006 we had distanced ourselves from our peers to become the largest infomercial company in Japan. We were ready to ascend to a new level.

TRULY BECOMING A *DAIHYO*

My employees taught me the true meaning of the title of *Daihyo-Torishimaruyaku*, the representative director or president and CEO. In Japan, however, the meaning is deeper. The *Daihyo* is the face of the organization. Over time, my employees made their expectations quite clear. As their representative, I was the face for all of them. I wasn't just Harry Hill. I was all of them and they were all part of me.

I started a dialog with my employees. What did they want from a president and CEO? How did I bring value to them both inside and outside the company? First and foremost, it became clear that they needed vision and purpose. Second, they told me they wanted me to be front and center. They wanted a leader. Someone who would not lead only the company but be a leader in the industry and the community. They also told me to look the part. A group of employees banded together to boldly tell me that they wanted me to upgrade my look, to be cooler and more fashionable. More on that later.

Creating a purpose-driven company was a theme that I had already internalized. Starting in 2005, we started a deliberate process to fully develop our vision, our mission and our values. The first decision we made was to define our guiding philosophy, our Profit-centric Tree (PCT). Using the image of an oak tree, our PCT model demanded that we create profit in order to deliver value to our five most important stakeholders:

- Our customers, to whom we delivered value through our products and services by enriching their lifestyles
- Our employees, who received value and profit through compensation and incentives, but also from a stable, purpose-driven work environment that provided growth opportunities
- Our business partners, who derived value and profit because we focused on fair, transparent and long-term business alliances
- Our society, because we obeyed the law, paid taxes, created jobs, made positive contributions to our community, and demonstrated leadership in our industry and through Corporate Social Responsibility (CSR) initiatives
- And finally, our shareholders, who reaped value through dividends and the steady growth of the company

We debated our vision for many months. We kept returning to the voice of our customers. When we did our job right, we provided products and services that made their everyday life easier and more enjoyable. We were enriching their lifestyles. And so, our shared vision became 'Enriching lifestyles worldwide.'

Vision or purpose is unchanging. The mission — how to best achieve the vision — is modified as circumstances change. For the most part, however, our mission through our Shop Japan branding process was to make profit by delivering products and services to our customers that made everyday life better.

We identified our five most important values: entrepreneurial spirit; diversity; continuous improvement; creativity; and Japanese-style hospitality, or *omotenashi*.

The management team had an excellent direction-setting dialog with our staff, and everyone bought into the concept. Most significantly, we put an end to the debate about what is more important, delivering profit to the company or value to the customer. This is a false equivalency. Both are important and not to be compromised.

At our annual Kickoff Meeting, and at our weekly meetings, we talked about and explained the PCT Philosophy, our vision, our mission and our values. They were more than words written on a piece of paper. We believed in these tenets, and we lived by them. As the representative of the company, it was my responsibility to lead consistently, based on our culture. It was incredibly powerful, but also quite demanding.

One of my proudest moments as a leader came when a group of employees approached me in early 2006. They explained that they felt our PCT Philosophy, vision, mission and values were a strong and meaningful promise by us, the corporation, to society. A promise they were proud of and believed in. They said they wanted to create a creed that would serve as the employees' promise to the company. So, they embarked on a year-long process to write the OLM creed and ten guiding questions. At the all-hands kickoff in 2007, we gave everyone a small card with the creed and ten questions, which we asked them to carry at all times while at work. Our culture defined us. We lived it and breathed it.

There are no leaders without followers. There are also leaders who have the title, but not the hearts and minds. And my experience also taught that there are leaders who have the hearts and minds, but not ethics or responsibility. We had successfully created a purpose-driven, profitable company.

I represented a motivated group. They made me more powerful. Our culture made us all more powerful.

When guests visited us in those years, all the employees would stand up to welcome them. It never failed to impress. They observed first-hand that our company operated at a higher than normal level of awareness and responsibility.

During this process of culture building, my secretarial section informed me that I needed to upgrade my look.

"You don't present yourself carefully enough," they said. I thought I looked good enough, and I was more concerned about the quality of my decisions than on impressing people with my appearance. Politely but firmly, my staff indicated that they expected more. "We want you to care about your appearance at all times," I was told. "Not only when you're in the office, but wherever you are, because you're never not representing us."

They were nice about it, but direct and forceful. "We want you to dress better. We want you to groom yourself better. We want you to be cognizant of how you appear and interact in public. And we're going to set some specific goals." One of these was for all of the men's fashion magazines to do an article on me. They wanted me to look 'cool and trendy,' and let the world see.

The truth of their concerns resonated with me the first time I went to Monte Carlo for the European Electronic Retail Convention, the annual trade show for television shopping companies worldwide. By then, we had established ourselves as one of the best infomercial companies anywhere.

It was one of my first trips to Europe, and I was shocked because Monte Carlo was just so cool! Everybody was fashionable, sporting expensive watches and other accessories. And I was just ... normal. I wore my conservative blue business suit. My shoes were ordinary. I looked OK, but I didn't stand out.

In my mind I was representing one of the top five companies in the industry, and one of the fastest growing. In terms of creating hit products, nobody in Japan was better than us. Japan was the third largest economy in the world. We were becoming royalty in our industry. Yet we didn't get that much notice.

Certainly, our performance merited attention. But our performance wasn't the problem. I wasn't wearing the uniform of success. I wasn't wearing a Brioni suit or sporting a Rolex watch. I wore work-a-day shoes, not Berlutis. I was overcome with my stupidity. "How can I be so wrong?" While decking myself out more stylishly might have seemed like a costly extravagance, if it helped us get the rights to just one more hit product, the return on investment would be exponential.

I believed that our story and our current performance should grab the attention of potential partners. Who else was selling tens or hundreds of million dollars of product in Japan? Of course, many companies noticed. But many also walked on by. I didn't look the part. Is that superficial? Were those companies making a mistake by not talking to me? Probably. I tried to convince myself that they were paying the price for their superficiality.

Bullshit!

Standing there amid the fabulous international buzz of Monte Carlo, the words of my secretarial team came back to haunt me. "You're **never** not representing us."

I made a change. I told my secretarial team to go for it. "I'm your canvas. Remake me. You want me to be featured in these fashion magazines as a 'cool' CEO? Make it so." They changed my barber. They hired a fashion consultant who would come to our house every two weeks. She would clean and press my clothes. Armed with my schedule, she'd arrange my outfits for the coming two weeks, for each and every day.

My look was planned for every meeting, media appearance or other occasion. She kept a detailed record of what I wore and never repeated a combination. Initially, she used the clothes I already owned. Over time, she told me what I should buy to supplement and enhance my wardrobe.

Almost immediately I had people, particularly women, randomly comment on my appearance, my fashion sense. Suddenly, people were paying compliments like, "Your style is so cool! Your sense of color is so good!" What was shocking to me was that my fashion consultant was initially using the clothes I already had, but arranged my outfits in ways that I would not have done on my own.

My transformation, which resulted in me being noticed more, and consequently helped the company attract attention, was a team effort. It would not have happened if I didn't have the right people on my secretarial team. They felt their job was more than simply supporting my schedule. Our company had a greater purpose. Their greater purpose was to empower me.

Most importantly, a representative director must lead. Globally, we had become recognized leaders of our industry. I became more visibly involved in our sector's professional groups and eventually became the first president of the Electronic Retailers Association who wasn't physically located in the US. We had set a goal to become number one and we'd succeeded. We were royalty in an industry where appearances mattered.

I also took on leadership roles in the non-profit world, in both the US and Japan. I was elected as a governor of the American Chamber of Commerce in Japan, in Nagoya and Tokyo, and assumed leadership of the non-profit HOPE International Development Agency Japan. I was appointed by the White House office of staffing as Chairman of the Japan-US Friendship Commission. We as a business took our role in making the industry and the world we lived in better quite seriously. So did I, personally. It was expected of me. I expected it of myself.

DISASTER STRIKES

A real test of our purpose and of my leadership came in the aftermath of 11 March, 2011, when the Tohoku region of Japan was hit by the triple disaster of earthquake, tsunami and nuclear accident.

It was a devastating day. I was holding a meeting with an outside vendor in my office in Nagoya. The earthquake shook us even there, more than 400 kilometers from the epicenter. Nagoya was not damaged, but Tokyo was badly affected. We had more than 100 employees in Tokyo, and Saturday and Sunday were primarily focused on making sure that all of them and their families were safe.

On 14 March, the company came together in person and remotely for our Monday morning weekly meeting. As you can imagine, this Monday was different.

All of Japan had been shaken, literally and emotionally. When I got up to speak, the employees looked at me expectantly, anxious to hear what I would say. I realized it was a critical moment to have our vision and values guide us. We always talked about giving to society, and at this moment, Japan, our home, was faced with a severe challenge.

I could see the questioning in my employees' eyes. "You talk about our vision, you talk about giving to society, you talk about our values," I could see them thinking. "Now, what are you going to do and how are you going to do it?" They really meant, "What are WE going to do?" Their expressions impressed upon me that this was a moment of truth. What do we stand for? What do we fight for?

We didn't hedge, we committed right away. We created the Genki Japan Fund. The non-profit I was chairman of, HOPE International Development Agency Japan, was primarily focused on digging wells to provide clean water to the poorest of the poor in Southeast Asia. Helping Japan as a nation in crisis was not part of the mandate. We changed the mandate.

As a company, we immediately donated ¥100 million and top management donated another ¥50 million. In the 12 months prior to the earthquake, we had bought approximately $150 million of products from suppliers outside Japan. I wrote to all of our suppliers declaring that it was a time of dire need, and asking them to donate 1% of what we had purchased the previous year. We took in more than $800,000 in donations. By 21 March, when I made my first inspection tour to the Tohoku region, the Genki Japan Fund had raised in excess of $2 million.

For the first several months, we partnered with an independent helicopter association to deliver emergency goods and services to remote locations. In visiting these places and talking with the people trying to rebuild their lives, I received a very clear message: "We don't want handouts. We don't want you to rebuild our homes. We need help and support in rebuilding our businesses, our ability to support ourselves. If we can rebuild our livelihoods, we will take responsibility for rebuilding our homes."

OLM was a purpose-driven company. We empowered people to sleep better, eat better, clean better. We helped them enrich their lives. We supported HOPE because it was a people-to-people non-profit that helped families change their lives by providing wells for clean water. Genki Japan funded 77 micro-projects that enabled people to either rebuild or start a business. It was 100% in line with our vision.

For the next several weeks, we conducted a daily meeting. Our first priority was to ensure the safety of our staff and their families. Our second was to ensure that our business continued to function and made a profit. Our third priority was to be an agent to rebuild Japan. Genki is the Japanese word for health. We made a difference. On that first Monday morning, as I stood in front of my team, their overriding expectation of me as a leader was clear: "Don't let us down."

BILLY'S BOOTCAMP, A SOCIAL PHENOMENON

Our annual sales in 2006, my first year as president and CEO, were just under ¥20 billion. That had more than doubled since deciding that Shop Jabranding was the core competency that would make us the top infomercial company in Japan.

We expected that being number one would allow us to improve in three key areas: attracting top talent; increasing brand and company awareness to boost sales and make it easier to conduct business; solidifying our product sourcing and procurement chain. By 2006 we were the home-shopping partner of choice in Japan for almost any supplier who had a hit product. We had made a transformation. Then the record-breaking success of Billy's Bootcamp took us to a whole higher level.

In 2007, we built and rode the wave of a pop-culture phenomenon. From January through September, we sold ¥19.5 billion worth of Billy's Bootcamp (BBC), a wildly popular set of four exercise DVDs. Billy Blanks, a Californian actor and fitness personality whose exercise program combined taekwondo and boxing, became an overnight celebrity in Japan, where he later married and took up residence. We created a craze that people still talk about, and doubled our sales in one year, to just under ¥40 billion. Our revenue from that single product in 2007 exceeded our previous greatest annual sales for the whole company. We were riding almost five years of momentum and confidence. We were #1.

There had been other iconic hits that stormed Japan through TV shopping. Before BBC, the Abtronic exercise device had been a raging success. The company that sold that item doubled their sales and leveraged the success for an IPO, only for sales and the share price to then crash back to Earth. The infomercial business is riddled with the remnants of companies that grow exponentially overnight and then fall back to, or tragically below, where they had started.

Even in the giddy months, as our sales and profit skyrocketed, we had eyes on our future. We didn't want to be just another has-been that couldn't sustain growth. We'd been preaching the concept of long-selling marketing and extending the life cycle of our products. Prior to the breakout with BBC, we had developed a stable core of brands. In essence, we kept maintaining the sales and profitability of our products while having a windfall with the DVD set. Its success greatly expanded our media and retail footprint. In 2008, our sales of BBC dropped from ¥19.5 billion to ¥900 million, about 0.5% of the sales of the previous year. Our company sales dropped ¥2.5 billion, just under 12%. The brands we'd been cultivating with our long-selling strategy filled the gap. In 2009, we exceeded ¥40 billion in revenue for the first time. We leveraged the success of BBC to grow company revenue 4.5 times from 2006 to 2016.

I am extraordinarily proud of this accomplishment. In the Japanese infomercial space, we were the first company to leverage the success of a major hit to become bigger, better and continue to grow.

The success of the exercise DVDs brought a whole new level of attention to our company. The product's brand awareness in Japan exceeded 80%. Indeed, it exceeded the brand awareness of Shop Japan itself, and our fame-by-association made it easier for us to do business. Good people were more interested in working for us, while our employees' pride in the company and motivation shot up. Vendors and media companies put their best people on our account. Our tremendous success with BBC became a talking point throughout the industry, worldwide. More and more, suppliers and brand owners sought us out to partner with in Japan.

You know by now how I love my lists of three. So, what are the three lessons that we learned from this experience?

The first was the importance of using momentum. The second is to prepare for the next phase of the journey, because a big hit never lasts. And the third is to make friends with other winners during times of success, with the goal of creating lasting relationships.

The BBC phenomenon almost never happened. Prior to our breakthrough, fitness DVDs in Japan had never succeeded. There had never been an instance of any company selling more than 20,000 copies of an exercise video. Remarkably, we sold more than 1.5 million four-DVD sets of BBC.

To put that in perspective, about 5% of Japanese households purchased BBC in 2007, so we obviously debunked the myth that Japanese people won't exercise in front of their TV. Once again we proved that despite deeply entrenched sociocultural assumptions, people are people, wherever you go.

Should this have been a surprise? In the US, home fitness videos and DVDs were a $1 billion a year business category. People had been exercising in front of their TVs since the 1950s, starting with Jack LaLanne, who hosted the longest-running syndicated exercise show in broadcast history, and booming again in the 1970s with Jane Fonda doing aerobics.

While the concept was not new, it had never caught on in Japan, even though others had tried. In fact, two other companies in Japan had tried and failed to sell BBC before we ran with it. But it fit our core criteria, and was a bonafide hit, proving that yes, people here were just like people everywhere.

We looked at what the previous companies had done and determined that the essential magic of the product had not been properly communicated. BBC was a major international hit. It was a social phenomenon in the US and Germany. There was a magic that Billy had, and we needed to tap into it.

We decided to test the market again with BBC based on our data-centric, rational evaluation of the product. If the fitness DVD market was $1 billion in the US, there should be the potential for it to be 30-40% of that in Japan. BBC was a worldwide megahit, and people of all ages loved working out with Billy. There was no reason he shouldn't resonate here.

The second lesson we learned was how fitness products had been marketed in Japan. Unlike the others that had been marginally successful, where the pitch was, "It's really easy, and you only have to do it 5-10 minutes a day," with BBC, we said up front that it wasn't going to be easy. "It takes an hour a day. You're going to feel sore. But you will absolutely get results." It broke the mold.

The third thing that we really focused on, and which became a theme of our company, was how it was fun.

People misunderstand the word fun, in that it doesn't necessarily mean 'Ha-ha!'

No. Fun is about the feeling we get when we feel we've accomplished something. Fun is about saying, "If I do this, I'll feel good about myself." Billy would end each work-out with, "Good job!" And the next thing we knew, people all over Japan were saying, "Gudo jobu." Not only did we change how people felt and looked, we added to their (sort of) English lexicon.

BBC allowed us to make our narrative Japan's narrative. In 2007, we contributed to all of Japan getting healthier.

Marketing giant Dentsu named us the third most influential brand in 2007, among all age groups. When we brought Billy to Japan for three days in June of that year, it became a media circus.

For the first two days after his arrival, we started at 5 am and finished after midnight, shuttling from TV station to TV station, appearing on both pre-recorded and live shows. In those couple of days, we sold 200,000 copies of BBC, worth more than ¥3 billion. We had the highest single-day sales in the history of the Rakuten e-commerce marketplace, which I believe still stands today.

Had we not brought Billy to Japan, it still would have been a major hit. Flying him over and mounting the publicity tour turned it from a major hit into a social phenomenon. By the time he left, everybody knew who Billy Blanks was, everybody knew BBC, and everyone knew Shop Japan, by what we did if not by name.

Prior to Billy's arrival in Japan, the product was on fire, and his visit poured gasoline on the fire. Riding momentum seems like an easy thing to do, but this was at a level none of us had seen before. We were a TV shopping company; we ran infomercials. And a lot of our programming aired at non-peak times — late at night, early in the morning — when the mainstream audience wasn't watching. We gauged response, and based on that data we would plan our media buy — the television time slots we would purchase to air our segments. Our business was to look for customer response, increase our media buy as the response crests, and decrease our spend when that response starts to wane. Our business was to create and ride waves.

What we saw in January of 2007 was an organic market-place response like none we'd ever seen before. It transcended our reach. If we normally saw sales in the order of 100 items per airing, we were now getting up to 4-5 times the volume.

In early 2007, the Japanese under-18 national soccer team were playing a game aired on national TV during prime time. The team performed the BBC exercise routine in the middle of the field after scoring their first goal. We had not orchestrated this; it reflected the extent to which BBC had caught fire and pervaded public consciousness. People all over Japan were using and talking about BBC. Our job was to fan the flames of the fire.

We hired a PR agency in February. I explained to them, "We've just rolled out this product, and we're seeing a response that we've never seen before. It's off the charts. We want to bring Billy to Japan in June, five months from now, to capitalize on this wave. We think we can take Japan by storm." I wanted to rent out the Tokyo Dome, have 40,000 people doing Billy's Bootcamp together, and have him make appearances on all the TV programs.

We presented my idea to the PR agency. They nodded their heads and said, "Let us come back to you with a plan."

Two weeks later they returned with a pessimistic reply: "This is just a TV shopping product. People who watch late-night TV may know about it, but it isn't really a mainstream thing. The popular TV programs will have no interest unless you pay them. And to rent out the Tokyo Dome costs ¥35 million (about $350,000 at the time). All you'll be doing is wasting your money."

We were seeing a record response and record profits, but my team was listening to the agency and losing confidence. The PR advisors basically said, "The notion that Billy's going to take Japan by storm is not tethered to reality. We can do some sort of appearances, but nothing at the level you're imagining. For you to spend that kind of money would be a bad idea."

We went back and forth, and I compromised a bit. Instead of renting the Tokyo Dome, we booked the Tokyo Dome Arena, which had 10% of the bigger stadium's capacity. Instead of 40,000 people, we could run an event with 4,000.

In the worst-case scenario, we had already achieved record sales and profits with BBC in a very short period of time. If all we did was run an event for our current customers who had purchased the product, our cost to bring Billy to Japan was already covered. We'd use house money to run an event for confirmed devotees, fan the flames of awareness and, of course, to increase sales.

I agreed to the plan for a smaller venue and, as the date of Billy's arrival drew closer, would wait and see what other opportunities would arise. The PR agency started to get excited when they saw that the Japanese media were showing interest in Billy's upcoming trip. Suddenly the mainstream media were approaching us with different types of shows and events while he was in Japan. However, most of these initial proposals came with a caveat: we had to work exclusively with that one media group. We were offered the opportunity to have Billy appear on some of the top-rated shows in Japan, which nobody says no to.

But that's precisely what we did.

We weren't interested in granting exclusive rights. As a TV shopping company, we relied on friendly relations and doing business with all the broadcast outlets. We didn't want to give the impression that we favored any one station.

And so, 72 hours prior to Billy's arrival, we had almost no confirmed appearances. Then, in a flash, all the broadcasters came back to us.

There are five major stations in Japan, and from the day after he arrived for two days, from early morning to midnight, we went from station to station. I don't remember all the different shows we were on. From the perspective of the everyday Japanese person, Billy seemed to be on every live TV show for two days straight. We had hijacked the Japanese media!

In those couple of days, we did $30 million in sales of fitness DVDs. It was just boom, boom, boom, boom. From that point on we rode the momentum. In the business of marketing and sales, there will be times when there's momentum, when riding the wave is incredibly important, and that requires courage. As we rode the tide of increased leverage and reach, the multiplier effect kicked in, growing the sales of our other products as well. The BBC phenomenon had a knock-on benefit to everything else we were doing.

If we had not been investing and pushing the momentum, we would not have doubled our business from fiscal 2006-2007. When we were riding the wave, taking some risks was a no-brainer because we had already made the money. We were using money in the bank to see whether we could push the envelope further, and we pushed it further than anybody had before.

Today, people still talk about Billy's Bootcamp. It put Shop Japan on the map, not just for our experience with those fitness DVDs but for everything we did.

And that's lesson number two. Prepare for what comes next.

There had been major hits in the direct marketing and TV shopping industry before. As I've said, we had seen companies riding a hit into orbit only to make a fiery re-entry.

We had sold $200 million worth of BBC in 2007. In 2008, sales of the same product were $900,000, a $199 million drop, yet our total sales as a company fell by only $25 million.

Why? Because we took the brands and the products that we had been slowly building for years and pushed them into the void left by the drop-off of our mega-hit product. There was a new, significantly bigger audience that was familiar with us, tuning in and buying what they saw, taking our company to a whole new level. We weren't simply reliant on a single hit product, we were building a stable of long-running offerings.

As an executive, I take more pride in our performance in 2008 than 2007. The year following the BBC explosion, 2008, showed that we could sustain our growth and momentum even without a social phenomenon like Billy lighting up the airwaves.

The final thing I learned was to make friends with winners. Suddenly, everybody knew who we were. We weren't the guerrilla marketers anymore. We weren't those late-night guys, the ones who do business in the off hours. We had captured the mainstream imagination. We had earned a place at the table and we leveraged that spot.

Having grabbed the spotlight, we became friendly with the leaders of some of the most influential companies in Japan. We had become one of them.

The great thing about winning is that winners want to hang out with other winners. If you become a champion, your name is preserved in history. And when we made those friends, it was incumbent on us to ensure that they stayed friends. People often ask if I ever imagined that we could create such a hit. The simple answer is 'yes.' I always believed our purpose was to change Japan, so when we found ourselves center-stage we weren't blinded by the lights. We had imagined this moment and we acted like we belonged. That enabled us to spread our wings in ways that we hadn't been able to before. From the perspective of a fighter, we had won a world title. Now it was time for us to prove it was no fluke.

SECOND SOCIAL PHENOMENON

The second big sensation we participated in was two-fold. We helped to change the perception of the direct-to-consumer brand storytelling industry and simultaneously became part of a wave of foreign-led corporations who were becoming part of the fabric of corporate Japan.

Becoming a purpose-driven company changed the vector of our business. We had a powerful 'why' for our business: enriching lifestyles by making everyday life fun and exciting. In Shop Jabranding we had a powerful 'how.'

'How' is the method we use to find and satisfy our customers. People would ask, "How can a portable vacuum cleaner be fun and exciting?" We found the answer from our customers. For instance, there was the 75-year-old woman who called us to say, "Thank you so much for the Swivel Sweeper. I can't get down on my knees and clean the way I used to. My vacuum cleaner is too heavy, and having difficulty using it made me feel old and bad about myself because I could no longer keep my home clean. Now I can!"

When we heard stories like this, we knew we were making a difference. These grassroots testimonials were our brand.

Our customers were always the star of our brand marketing. We had a powerful 'how.'

Increasingly, major brands approached us to learn how we did business and to explore the potential to collaborate. The interest in our company sometimes felt somewhat ironic. For as long as I had been involved with OLM, direct marketing, TV shopping and particularly infomercials had been the punchline of jokes. We were the poor stepchild of the branding and marketing industry. Now, like Cinderella coming out of the shadows, our potential was revealed.

The Japan president of a major cosmetics company asked me to meet with his headquarters management group in the US to explore a possible joint venture on some of their newly developed products. I made a presentation to a C-Level group representing each of the major brands from this conglomerate. They thought what we were doing was cool because we were talking directly to our customers. They thought it was fun and exciting. The meeting was very positive.

Then, one executive raised her hand and asked, "You aren't talking about infomercials, are you?" And suddenly the mood in the room deflated. It was like their collective attitude was, "We don't do TV shopping. That's not consistent with our brand image or our values." Somehow how we did business was more important than the 'why.'

Every one of those cosmetics brands, and the larger group they were a part of, liked our approach to brand storytelling, but the idea that it could be done through TV shopping shook them. I realized that what we had done with BBC was to transcend this idea, at least in Japan, that a direct marketing company or TV shopping company was about second-tier products rather than mainstream brands. We had done that by becoming the third-most influential brand ourselves in Japan for 2007. For us, mainstream or second-tier didn't matter. We were focused on our purpose, and we wanted to use the best means to fulfil that purpose profitably. If we served a purpose and made a profit, we had achieved our mission.

People outside our industry started looking at working with us and taking a new approach to reaching their customers. While we were transcending the reach and scope of the infomercial, other companies were greatly expanding the reach and influence of live shopping. In a short period of time, the genre became mainstream. On the infomercial side, this was mainly achieved by us.

Our brand storytelling marketing method, incorporating a direct conversation with the consumer, was changing the narrative. In the brand marketing world, often the brand was the hero. We were making the everyday person the hero. Using James Bond as an example, it isn't the Aston Martin that makes Bond cool. Rather, it is 007 driving an Aston Martin that gives the car its appeal. Our approach was to make all of our customers the 007 of their lives.

We were influencing the way brands would communicate with their customers. As trailblazers, more and more companies engaged with us. Several large brands wanted to explore how they could communicate directly with their customers by working with us.

We went from being seen as outside the mainstream to representing a new and exciting alternative branding strategy. We were one of a handful of innovators who influenced a change in the way companies interacted and communicated with their consumers. From the TV shopping side, we were one of the group of four in Japan — the others being Japanet Takada, Shop Channel and QVC — that made TV shopping part of the everyday experience. And in that group, we were the only infomercial company.

By focusing on authentic testimonials, we were a forerunner to the trend of user-generated content (UGC).

We increasingly planned a media mix to drive interest and sales to multiple points of sale, including our call centers, e-commerce sites, as well as bricks and mortar retail locations. As a data-driven company, we could see an increase in sales across all channels as we increased our touch points.

One new acquaintance, the CEO of a luxury brand, explained his dilemma as follows: "Our main strategy is to have a few flagship locations in major metropolitan areas, but our primary sales channel is stores within the major department stores. According to our data, our in-store conversion is going up, but our traffic is down because the traffic to department stores is down. We're more effective in sales, but less effective in driving traffic because we essentially outsourced creating traffic to the big-box retailers. Now we have to devote more resources to driving traffic ourselves."

I heard variations on this theme from our new circle of contacts. The Japanese corporate world, particularly Japan-based foreign CEOs, were fascinated by what we had achieved, first with Billy's Bootcamp, and subsequently with the steady growth of our other product brands. They were interested in learning from us or partnering with us. TV shopping and direct-to-consumer brand storytelling was to them a new revelation.

Our emergence from the shadows of the midnight hours also made us more valuable as a company. This ultimately resulted in NTT Docomo, a Japanese mobile phone operator, purchasing a majority interest in OLM in April of 2009. It was one of the largest domestic M&A transactions that year.

Robert and Nakamura had explored several potential growth and exit scenarios for OLM. Prior to my joining in 1999, they had secured outside investment and had started the process of a potential IPO. As I explained earlier, this preparation was premature, but it created the environment for our rebirth.

From 2004-2006, we were approached by several companies about a potential merger or capital alliance. Robert was in the process of moving to China, so both he and Nakamura, as they were ceding day-to-day control to me, were interested in a partial exit and monetization of their shares. We had serious conversations with several companies, including one major trading company that approached us in 2005.

At the first meeting they offered a valuation of ¥12.5 billion, subject to due diligence. We negotiated with them for about six months, and it became clear that they were using the due diligence process to two self-serving ends: to get a free education on how we did business and with whom, and as a weaponized process to drive the purchase price down.

Our last meeting with them was the most memorable. We had the final version of the contract. Based on their skewed due diligence, they had whittled down the valuation. Nevertheless, Robert and Nakumura, the two primary shareholders, were on the verge of accepting. We had what we thought was going to be the last meeting to finalize the agreement. The other party asked for us to host the meeting at our attorney's office. Our corporate lawyer was a well known American partner of one of the leading international law offices in Japan, a veteran of numerous M&A transactions (including with the company with which we were negotiating) and a trusted mentor and friend to Robert and me. Robert was in China, and I was tasked with closing the deal.

The other side arrived in a group of seven people for our meeting. Our attorney had reserved a conference room in his firm's offices. He and I sat down on one side of the table, and they sat down on the other. The other side then objected. They had not brought an attorney. Although the meeting was at our attorney's office, they said they didn't know we would be bringing an attorney. Of course, he had been involved in the contract negotiations leading up to this point — and this was the formal closing of a major equity agreement, after all — so their objection was curious.

Our attorney exploded. He recommended that we cancel the meeting. He advised that I should not accede to these underhanded tactics. I had already made up my mind. I told him not to worry, I could handle the meeting myself. Reluctantly, he left the room. I sat on one side. The seven of them sat on the other. This was a group that had wined and dined me. We had become friendly in a business-relationship sort of way. I asked, "How many of you majored in law at university?" Four of them responded affirmatively.

I excused myself from the room. I went into our attorney's office and we called Robert and Nakamura. I appraised them of the situation and made my recommendation for us to walk away. Robert and Nakamura concurred. If we weren't going to be treated with respect, we knew that a partnership had no prospect for success.

I returned to the room, thanked the company for their interest in us, and informed them that we were no longer interested in partnering with their company.

I left the room. It had become perfectly clear that they were not negotiating with us in good faith or from a position of respect. Based on our interactions, we lost all confidence that we could work with this company to create synergy and increase the value of OLM. I later heard that the lead negotiator on the other side lost his job for failing to deliver the deal.

Less than four years later, we closed the deal with NTT Docomo for a market valuation in excess of 4x what the trading company had offered. They had been right to see value in us, but their greed and underhanded dealings upended the deal. I suspect that if we had done the deal with them, they would have hindered our next level of growth, so in every respect I think we won by walking away. From a fighter's perspective, it is essential to walk away from any fight if the rules appear to be stacked against you.

Post-Billy, we were given a whole new level of respect. In 2008, we once again explored the concept of both a cash and strategic merger with a larger entity.

Some asked why we entertained this idea when we were growing and making money. We put together a strong investment package. We had a clear three-year growth strategy for 2009-2011. Just as we finished our package, the financial giant Lehman Brothers, which was $613 billion in debt, filed for bankruptcy, sending the already recessionary global economy into a tailspin. That supercharged Robert's, and especially Nakamura's, desire to monetize some of their OLM shares, to diversify their holdings.

This was just after our huge growth with Billy's Bootcamp, and our annual turnover had increased from about $150 million to almost $400 million. We had a strong team and a great way of doing business. We had created value.

OPPORTUNITY AND RISK

While we had a clear path forward for the next several years, we saw many uncertainties in the near future. One of the key strengths of our company was the ability to identify and monetize undervalued media, particularly TV programming. We knew that in 2011, when Japan converted from analog terrestrial television broadcasting to the digital platform, the value of media would change. The change would bring opportunity, but it also meant that our existing data on the value of legacy media would need to be recalibrated. The emergence of mobile handsets and mobile internet (this was pre-iPhone) also meant that the way the public consumed and responded to media was changing. We saw both opportunity and risk. Bringing in an outside synergistic partner seemed an ideal solution to both maximize opportunity and to mitigate risk.

Shinsei Bank became our manager and shopped the deal to several companies. We entertained offers, but ultimately narrowed down the finalists to three contenders: a private equity firm, a large trading company, and NTT Docomo. Based on both the value and potential synergy they brought to the table, we chose NTT Docomo (that second part stands for 'do communications over the mobile network' as *dokomo* in Japanese also means everywhere) as our partner. We initiated exclusive negotiations with them in the fall of 2008 and closed the deal at the beginning of April 2009. I believe it was the fifth-biggest M&A deal in Japan that calendar year.

Two major shifts of perspective came with them becoming majority owner of Oak Lawn Marketing and Shop Japan. The infomercial industry now had a firm stamp of approval from Japan Inc., and from a respected mainstream telecom company that had formerly been part of the government.

Infomercials were no longer the poor stepchild of the branding and marketing arena. Now even mainstream companies — and NTT, Nippon Telegraph and Telephone, were the epitome of mainstream — were indicating, "We need to be part of this. We need to have this type of communication. We want this kind of company in our corporate group."

QVC and Shop Channel, two of the biggest live TV shopping operations, were run by two major Japanese trading companies. Now OLM/Shop Japan, the largest infomercial company, was part of the NTT Docomo group. TV shopping and direct marketing had definitively moved out of the shadows.

The second major change in perspective was that this most blue-chip of blue-chip Japanese companies bought what was technically a foreign-owned (more than 50% of OLM's shares were owned by non-Japanese individuals), foreign-run company, and kept a non-Japanese Westerner as the CEO. This was not a merger between corporate giants like Mitsubishi Trading and QVC to create QVC Japan, or Sumitomo Trading and Shop Channel to create

Jupiter Shop Channel. This was Japan Inc. buying a made-in-Japan company from a foreign entrepreneur (Robert) with a Japanese partner (Nakamura), and leaving the chief executive, me, in place.

For the next eight years, Oak Lawn Marketing/Shop Japan was NTT Docomo's most successful non-core investment in terms of revenue and profit.

In 1990, I had to create my own company in order to be employed, because Japanese companies weren't interested in a Japan-hand's hybrid skills. This was true for Robert, myself and others of our ilk. The Japan generalist was not seen as valuable to a mainstream Japanese company. They had been looking for a specific expertise to rent for 3-5 years, and then send us on our way. Now, foreigners like us, who had invested decades in becoming experts in doing business in Japan, were promoted and featured within the system. We were no longer outsiders in the same way that we were in the 1990s. We had become part of the fabric of Japanese society.

So, we helped spearhead two paradigm shifts.

Billy's Bootcamp was disruptive. It changed how people saw the infomercial. We were part of the growing acceptance of TV shopping and direct marketing as a viable method of branding and interacting with customers. While participating in the full legitimization of our industry, we also helped normalize the idea that a non-Japanese person could understand and successfully lead a major company, as part of mainstream Japan Inc. We had gained the respect of our peers and the general public.

BBC put us on the map. By continuing to perform and lead, by continuing to stand for something, we were part of the disruption of corporate Japan, to everyone's benefit. We went from being consummate outsiders to influencing from the inside.

Post-Billy and post-merger with NTT Docomo, we were increasingly recognized as a leading company. We were not small by any means, but we punched above our weight. We had broken through the *gaijin* (foreigner) ceiling and were afforded respect and a place at the table both with corporate Japan and among multinational firms. We were featured in the Japanese media. I appeared on TV as one of the *Zettai Ni Shite-okitai Nijunin* — 20 People in Japan You Should Know. I was written up in business magazines, general interest publications, trade journals, fashion magazines and fighting magazines.

Becoming a purpose- and profit-driven company had started our change. Creating our Shop Jabranding process had codified how we did business. Our PCT Philosophy, PCT Credo, the ten questions and our organizational values guided our hiring and operations. We were young, energetic, confident and successful.

TRUE BELIEVERS: PASSION TO WOW

Our next stage as a purpose-driven company was to focus even more closely on our customer. We created two initiatives, 'Walk the Talk' and 'Passion to Wow,' to power our growth. As we focused on these programs, we kept three concepts as the basis for our planning:

One, never to stray from our purpose to identify and resolve a 'complex,' to enrich lifestyles.

Two, never to be content with being normal or just good enough.

Three, never to be satisfied with the status quo. Peaks and valleys were an inevitable part of our business. Planning for the next downturn, and constantly searching for innovation both in what we sold and how we did business, were essential to our survival.

Let's look at those three things, and the 'Walk the Talk' initiative.

When we talked about enriching lifestyles, about changing people's lives through our products, it meant that we had to stand in our customer's shoes, understand their dilemma and fully empathize with the process of solving it.

We had to live and breathe our brands. Since we generally didn't develop our own products, we had to find best-in-class companies to partner with and learn from.

One of the best examples of me learning how to live and breathe a brand was in the negotiation and successful rollout of Bare Escentuals. At the time, this was the number-one line of mineral-based makeup and skincare products in the US. They had hired a consultant to identify the best partner for them in Japan, who approached us. Our negotiations took almost a year. Within 12 months of launching the infomercial, BareMinerals was the top mineral-based cosmetics brand in Japan.

Near the conclusion of the negotiations, my team and I were in San Francisco to finalize the partnership. At the first meeting with their CEO, one of the best-known US cosmetics executives, she gave us all gifts. I was given a package of men's skincare products. I had to hide my ignorance. Up until then, I had never really used anything other than a generic bar of soap. Yet, here I was trying to negotiate this major deal with a prestigious cosmetic skincare brand. I had studied the opportunity on paper, but I was not a user.

From then on, I not only studied the business opportunity and the brand, but made a promise to myself to be a user, even with products that didn't necessarily fit my profile. Walking the talk is about leading by example. And we tried to make this true for everybody in our company.

As a male in my 40s, it felt unnatural to suddenly be changing my daily grooming routine. But now, my new morning ritual at home was to knead and massage my face and neck with skin cream and moisturizer. This was more than a little embarrassing. I was doing it covertly, when Yumiko was either still asleep or upstairs. I didn't want her saying, "What are you doing? You've never done this before!"

After I'd been following this routine for a couple of weeks, she woke up, looked at me one morning and said, "Harry, are you getting younger?"

In that moment, I viscerally felt the value of the product, the ritual and the results. I got it. This is what we do. We give our customers the tools to feel and look better in ways that are demonstrable, that people around them will notice. I knew if we could get the average customer, female or male, to try the product for a few weeks and have someone comment that they looked younger, that would be solid gold! That's how we make money. We would delight our customers. That's purpose and profit. That's what we do.

When the customer truly expresses, "This happened to me, this is how I felt," that's living the brand. As a company, we felt that it was important for as many of us as possible to live our brands, not just as casual users but as true believers. Not that we weren't already doing this, whether it was with fitness products, cleaning products, or whatever, but this skincare experience reinforced in my mind the power of the story. We had to experience our products and brands like our customers did.

We needed to transcend 'selling.' Our job was to help our customers define a problem, an itch, that they perhaps had trouble identifying or entirely understanding, and then provide the means to scratch the itch. We understood that people are people. We suffer from the same quirks and complexes as our customers. It was incumbent on all of us to be users, so that we could fully empathize with them.

It brought additional focus, and we spent years internally encouraging everyone in the company to be users, to truly become lovers of our products and services. Of course, some of our offerings weren't meant for everybody, but this collective mindset allowed us to stay laser-focused on the customer.

We created two mechanisms to better capture and turn our experiences into data: VOC (Voice of Customer) and VOE (Voice of Employee).

We had always used customer testimonials, but now we created a deeper process to capture their voices, whether bad or good. Listening discerningly took practice and precision and we worked closely with our call center to turn words into data.

Turning words, particularly complaints, into data points is important because we have to be careful not to be distracted by the loudest, most recent or unhappiest voice. On any given day, somebody is going to be mad at us about something, and sometimes it's simply because they're having a bad day. That's why we needed to quantify the data and differentiate between consistent issues and one-off complaints. Our call centers took more than three million calls a year. We learned to find the signals through the noise.

The VOC process we created empowered the opinions of our call center employees, the communicators who represented our company to the outside world. A full-time communicator talked directly with thousands of our customers each year. They would speak with more customers than me, the CEO, so in many ways they were the most important voice of the company to this most important audience. They also often represented the same raw demographics as the people who were buying our products. So, we saw our communicators as both an extension of our company and an extension of our customers. Better amplifying their voice was our expression of gratitude for the work they did and respect for their opinions.

The VOC was an extension of the process of learning from our customers, and it helped us continue to extend the life cycle of our products. By staying in touch with our customers, we honed our marketing message, to create better shows and to better identify ways to improve the quality and usability of our products.

The VOC drove results and increased motivation. Meanwhile, we created the VOE to give the same type of empowerment to our full-time employees.

Our purpose was to 'enrich lifestyles,' not just for our customers but for all of our stakeholders. As Shop Japan, our customer-facing store, our purpose was to address people's everyday complexes — those personal thoughts and impulses that can affect confidence and well-being — by giving them the tools to look and feel better about themselves. With the VOE, we focused on making the work environment better.

Both VOC and VOE became important mechanisms for us to identify problems and search for solutions. They reflected us internalizing the thought, "I identify with that problem, that person, that complex. I want that solution." Since Shop Jabranding was about storytelling, we tried to turn everything into stories that illustrated a problem and a solution. This was our approach both inside and outside the company. When we were running in sync, it was a powerful process.

Walking the talk, living the brand, VOC and VOE made us think deeply about our workplace environment. How did we enable our employees to be fulfilled and motivated, both at work and outside of the office? Most of our products and services were 'at home' solutions. So, if our employees are ultimately an extension of our customers, how do we provide an environment where they can grow and feel satisfied both at work and home? For me, as the leader of a company that was walking the talk, this focus was essential for us to have credibility with our employees (so they too could walk the talk) and in society. We treated our employees and our customers the way we expected other companies to behave.

"If we're not giving our employees time away from the office and the ability to actually live this enriched lifestyle, how can they possibly communicate that to our customers?"

Our purpose truly allowed us to aim higher. Our products and brands were household names. As mentioned earlier, the Japanese Cabinet recognized me as a 'Male Champion of Change' for our diverse work environment and empowering of women. We sat at the table as equals with the CEOs of top domestic and non-Japanese companies because of what we stood for and how we did business. Purpose combined with profit gave us influence.

Our purpose was to empower the individual — our customers, our communicators, our employees. Our vision was to enrich their lifestyles.

Our response to the March 2011 earthquake, tsunami and nuclear meltdown was representative of our philosophy. We didn't just contribute to a non-profit relief group, we partnered with HOPE Japan to ensure that the funds were used to empower individuals.

As noted, the people of Tohoku, who were most severely affected by the disaster, said to us quite clearly, "We can rebuild our own homes. Help us rebuild our businesses." And that's what we did.

This was completely consistent with walking the talk. We were empowering individuals to be the best they could be by helping them rebuild their livelihoods.

There is another example of our choice to be different. For several months following that triple disaster, Japan was overwhelmed, and focused on *jishuku*, the notion that everyone should cut back and suffer with the people of Tohoku.

As part of this group empathy movement, almost all companies voluntarily stopped airing commercials, particularly in Tohoku. We ritually dimmed the lights. Across Japan, everyone was cutting consumption.

In many ways, this was a precursor to COVID-19, in terms of the expectation that we should all suffer together.

As we were doing our part with the Genki Japan Fund, we made the decision that, contrary to what other companies were doing, we would conduct business as normal. This was in fact altruistic, in that we needed to make money so we could do our part in helping the people affected by the disaster.

We were one of the first to re-start advertising after the disaster, in Tohoku and across Japan. We created a script at the call center to respond to anybody who called in to complain that we weren't respecting Japan's time of collective pain. And call they did. "You should be ashamed of yourself," we heard. "This is a time for restraint." Our communicators' talking points explained what we were doing in Tohoku, about the money we were providing to assist people in re-starting businesses, and that we'd chosen to actively conduct business because we felt that was the best way for us to help.

That script generally satisfied everybody who called. And it was noteworthy that we didn't receive any complaints from the people of Tohoku. Rather, the calls we got from there — sometimes from people in evacuation centers and shelters — were all positive. "Thank you. Everybody else has forgotten us," they said. "You still care."

People were thanking us simply for airing our commercials, for treating the region normally, as if it still mattered. In fact, displaced people were soon ordering products that we'd deliver to them in shelters and evacuation centers. We conducted business as usual, which helped people get back to normal.

In walking the talk, we stood for something and empowered the individual. And because we stood for something, it made a difference. This allowed us to not only compel the best and the brightest companies to want to do business with us, but it also allowed us to retain and attract top talent who believed in our vision to make everyday life better for the ordinary person.

Our second catchphrase was 'Passion to Wow.' We became well known for surprising and delighting. The heart of any good story, including an infomercial brand story, is the big reveal, where the problem is overcome and the heroine or hero lives happily ever after. It's more than just a before-and-after. We called it BAA: before-after-after. I had an issue, I resolved my complex, and now my life has changed for the better.

These are Wow moments and Wow stories. We became experts at creating these stories. That meant we had to deliver on our promise with our products and services. It required us to engage and connect with our customers. It's so much easier to just focus on the product or brand. That is completely in corporate control. How the customers use our product to change their lives was riskier. We offered no miracle solutions. All of our products required our customers to do the work.

Passion to Wow became part of our mission. I always felt that in some ways Billy's Bootcamp was a lost opportunity. We inspired and touched all of Japan, but we burned too bright and too fast. The Billy boom flamed out faster than it should have. By pursuing a more sustained Wow factor, we could have maintained our momentum for much longer.

Another great storyline we created was the Hills Diet Grand Prix. It was a hybrid between an infomercial and reality TV. For several years, it made the Hill's Diet meal replacement brand one of the most successful diet programs in Japan, even as cheap copycat products flooded the market. Our shows were particularly inspiring for middle-aged and older women. We were more than a product.

We were a lifestyle guide. And our customers related to the stories. Like the mother who didn't want to be photographed with her children because she didn't want a reminder of how she looked. She revealed that Hill's Diet gave her back her family and her smile.

We had so many unscripted, real moments that wowed and inspired our customers, and touched all of us at OLM. For the right audience, we were must-see TV.

At our best, we identified a customer base and then transcended the reach of the infomercial by exploiting all channels relevant to the customer demographic we'd pinpointed. The Wonder Core craze was the most representative of this approach. Wonder Core was a simple-to-understand exercise product that focused on core muscles, particularly strengthening the abdominals and lower back. The infomercial was rolling out successfully, and in its first year, Wonder Core sold about the same number of units as Billy's Bootcamp. But unlike BBC, we were able to sustain those sales over a three-year period. The Wonder Core series of products sold more than six million units. That amounted to 15% penetration of all Japanese households. We created a 30-second commercial message that caught worldwide attention for being fun and unique. But it also clearly explained the unique sales point of the product. Wonder Core brought surprise and delight. It wowed in all respects, including through customer satisfaction and, for us, sales and profit.

We went beyond normal. We created Wow moments. We wanted our customers and staff to believe that doing a little bit extra mattered.

THE TRUE SLEEPER INCIDENT

Our experience with the True Sleeper product inspired me to adopt a practice of visiting China twice a year, to visit our primary manufacturers. Whenever we went, the factories would get nervous. They believed the only reasons for corporate executives to visit were to negotiate a lower price, faster lead times, better quality, or all three. That was the norm.

When I met with our suppliers, I acknowledged that price, lead time and quality would always be a topic. However, I would add that our focus was on creating relationships, partnerships that were fair and beneficial to all parties. I wanted to visit our primary factories at least once per year to show respect and say 'thank you' on behalf of our company and our customers. A single, perfunctory visit didn't yield trust or results. Annual visits ultimately did.

What happened with the True Sleeper memory foam mattress could have been disastrous for our reputation, but instead it earned us greater trust from our customers.

The problem started when our VOC mechanism reported that some customers were complaining of discovering dead insects in the True Sleeper packaging.

We quickly ascertained that this issue started peaking as the weather turned warmer. We sent our quality assurance specialists to the Chinese factory, and they discovered that the facility had insufficient air conditioning, so they kept the windows open. However, some of the windows lacked insect screens. So, we invested in upgrading the air circulation system and screening all the windows. We made the work environment for this manufacturer better, while addressing the customer satisfaction issue.

This was during a time of high political tension between China and Japan. Several months after we'd invested in the upgrades, a disgruntled employee at this same factory sabotaged several mattresses by concealing sewing pins inside, and wrote 'Fuck Japan' inside other packages.

Any health- or safety-related customer claim was immediately escalated. We were quickly able to identify the lot and batch of the products that might have been affected. In turn, the factory was able to identify the employee, and control the situation on their end. We then had to immediately contact several thousand potentially impacted customers so that we could inspect and, as necessary, replace their product. As a direct marketing company, we had our customers' contact information, so we managed to reach almost everyone in the affected group within several days of identifying the problem. However, a three-day weekend was approaching, and there were still 30 or so customers who we'd been unable to contact.

We established a command center and sent out teams of 2-3 employees to physically visit the customers. We went beyond what one would expect, bringing in electronic sensors to inspect all the products in question. None of the customers complained about the intrusion or inconvenience. We were prepared for people to be angry or to lose trust in us. Instead, the response was exactly the opposite.

"We appreciate your approach to the problem," we were told. "Instead of trying to sugar-coat this or hide it, you came to tell us about it and fix it."

Our employees came back with *omiyage* (souvenirs), and reported how meeting customers ended up being some of the most meaningful moments they'd had working for Shop Japan. Potential disaster averted. And the goodwill that we got from our actions inspired us.

By standing for something, not being content to be normal, and saying, "Our focus is to wow people, to go beyond what's necessary," we earned our customers' trust. That singular focus helped us create a new wave of growth, which lasted until right after the Wonder Core years.

By regularly visiting all of our main manufacturers in China, I wanted these partners' management and employees to see that we were real, and not some faceless, uncaring foreign entity. We cared about them, and we expected them to care for us. They weren't just a replaceable third party vendor. We focused on creating a special relationship, a deep bond in our business dealings. Over the years, these bonds would be essential for us.

One morning in early April of 2014, I checked my email as usual as soon as I woke up. There was an urgent "Call me immediately!" note. The message was from the sales representative of the company that was supplying our best-selling home fitness product at the time.

He informed me that his company, the product owner, had filed for bankruptcy. We had just begun our new fiscal year, which would run to the following March, for which we'd forecast more than $100 million in sales of that product alone.

The sales rep was the son of the founder of the company, who had already sold the business. Over the years, the son and I had become close. In many ways I had acted as a mentor and older brother to him. He understood that a disruption in the supply chain, and losing the ability to sell this fitness product, would have catastrophic consequences for us.

He was calling both out of concern and with a proposal for us to immediately purchase the intellectual property rights for the exercise device, which would allow us to continue selling it regardless of the supplier's bankruptcy proceedings. We immediately coordinated a plan of action to protect OLM.

The sales rep was, and remains, very similar to me. He pursues business for the dual goals of making money and serving a purpose. He also believes in relationships. He chose to do business with OLM because we shared his values. We connected on a deeper level than simple profit. He believes in karma. He was our trusted salesman, and he was going to ensure that to his last breath he would satisfy his commitment to us. That was the type of relationship we had built. That was the type of loyalty we gave and received.

We sorted out the issue of rights and ownership, but my friend was still deeply troubled. His company had an outstanding purchase order for close to $8 million with their manufacturer in the Chinese city of Xiamen. The payment terms were FOB (Freight on Board). The bankruptcy meant that his company would neither accept nor pay for the outstanding order. My friend was fairly certain that the Chinese manufacturer would not survive. So, securing the intellectual property rights for the product was only half the problem. If the manufacturer failed, it would take us 6-8 months at a minimum to find a replacement factory. We would lose the sales window, particularly between April and September, when we expected to realize the majority of our sales. My friend had a special relationship with the CEO of the Chinese manufacturer, and arranged for us to meet.

Ultimately, there are very few decisions that are solely the CEO's to make. Most of our major successes came from me empowering my employees to achieve great things. There were a few cases, however, where responsibility rested squarely with me. These were immensely risky decisions that only I would take the blame for should they not work out.

My team and I immediately contacted the Chinese manufacturer and determined that they had an immediate cash need of about $2 million. With an infusion of cash, they felt they could take the product they'd manufactured on behalf of the US supplier that had gone bankrupt, sell it on the open market and return to financial viability. They had an aggressive plan of action, but they needed the money by week's end.

We sent the money as a pre-payment for future products. Had they failed, we wouldn't have been able to sell Leg Magic for that anticipated $100 million top line and $10-15 million bottom line. We had a dilemma. Should we risk $2 million for the sake of preserving this business? That was a decision that was mine, and only mine, to make. I made a recommendation to our board that we should help this company, pending our staff verifying the situation, but my credibility was at stake.

My staff spent the week at the Chinese manufacturer. They were convinced that the company could turn the corner. They convinced me. We sent the money. We experienced no disruption in the supply chain. The product continued to be a major hit. We sold more than we'd forecast. Our profitability was strong. Within eight months the manufacturer had recouped most of their costs. They had shipped over $100 million worth of product to us, fully delivering the pre-paid order. And, they had returned to financial health.

The next year, I made my annual factory visits to China. The Leg Magic factory was my first stop. Over three years, we had purchased more than five million of the devices from them. A black limousine picked up our entourage from Xiamen Airport. As we approached the entrance to the factory, the driver suddenly rolled down the windows.

We turned through the gate onto an internal service road, several hundred meters long, leading to the entrance-way to the main factory. All the employees — more than 2,000 people — lined both sides of the road.

"Thank you, Oak Lawn Marketing," they shouted. "Thank you, Mr. Harry!" The words were chanted over and over. The sound was deafening, the energy overwhelming. The limousine stopped at the entrance to the factory. The CEO and his management team were waiting. I stepped out of the car to raucous cheers. They had erected a commemorative rock in the garden outside the front door to celebrate five million units sold, and the undying friendship between our two companies.

While five million units is impressive, I know that they had fulfilled larger orders to other companies. Yet, ours may have been the most important order they'd ever fulfilled because it helped them survive. It was an incredibly touching scene.

As a fighter, I've learned that sometimes you need to do everything in your power to hang on. You have to figure out how to survive in order to find a way to compete. I knew from experience what it was like to get up off the canvas, in order to compete in the later rounds. We helped this company get to the later rounds. And for that, we had a friend for life.

Over the years, this Chinese manufacturer would be a trusted partner and friend. On several occasions when we encountered quality issues with fitness products at other manufacturing facilities, they went the extra mile to help us find a solution.

We made a calculated decision to try to preserve this line of business. We did not try to extract an exorbitant penalty. It was a good business decision that appeared altruistic, but was simply enlightened self-interest. Perhaps we could have extracted more, but then the only return on this investment would have been the immediate benefit we derived. Generosity ultimately created friendship, better performance and a higher return over the long haul.

We took a calculated risk. We believed in integrity and the power of relationships. Had we taken an alternate course, we would have failed to make budget and potentially would have lost money. Our investment in relationships, staying true to our PCT Philosophy, maximized our return.

At the crest of this wave, in November of 2015, when everything was peaking, I went back into the ring, as detailed in the prologue of this book. My previous fight had been in March of 2012, as an exhibition charity match at a professional event in Nagoya. This time I would fight as the main event, at a black-tie gala at a prestigious hall in Tokyo.

My fight was featured in GQ magazine. Yahoo! reported on the event. The way I lived and led was featured on a 2016 New Year's TV variety show featuring six of the top CEOs in Japan.

We were a Wow company. I was a Wow CEO. We had hit a peak in sales, with strong profitability. Our company commanded respect, both domestically and internationally. We were the leading NTT Docomo subsidiary, an internal star that they pointed to among the various companies they'd invested in. We seemed to be on top of the world.

But as we had learned before, waves crest and recede. Bubbles burst. This was something we were about to experience again.

That doesn't always mean that the underlying fundamentals aren't sound. It doesn't mean that a company's culture is suddenly irrelevant or the team suddenly unable to perform. But each business contraction is a time to refocus and rebuild. Since bubbles burst, we always have to be preparing for the next step. Today's best practice is tomorrow's normal operating procedure. And maybe it will become the future's extinct practice. Circa 2000, and in 2011, and now again at the end of 2016 and beginning of 2017, we were at a crossroads, confronted with an existential threat. It wasn't a question of why we do business, but how we do business.

The Shop Japan customer, the person who watched TV infomercials, was aging. We were not attracting as many customers through our traditional means of acquiring them, via direct response television. Many of our products and services had a general appeal to a wide base of the Japanese population — Billy's Bootcamp and Wonder Core, for example, were hits across all demographics — but we had not found reliable new means of communication to reach a wider audience. We were becoming the sales and marketing company for the silver-haired generation. Not a problem per se, but our best-case scenario seemed to be that we'd become gradually smaller rather than continue to grow.

This was the third major recession in the 18 years I had been at OLM. Like the previous times, three things happened.

First, the company had too much overhead. We hired aggressively for growth, but we were now contracting rather than growing. We had too many people, producing too little.

Second, we had too many initiatives. We were trying to expand and diversify the way we did business, but instead we were losing focus. We were spreading our best talent too thin, and rather than hedging our risks through diversification, we were simply diluting performance across too many areas of business. We'd lost focus and the new initiatives were not working.

And third, we faced a changing business environment. Failed initiatives and a changing landscape are often quite related. We needed to continue to experiment and challenge, but a string of failed initiatives had created an atmosphere where people were fearful of trying new things.

I was worried. Perhaps too much success had dulled my ability and will to fight. It certainly had dulled my vision.

MY VISION FAILS ME

We entered the 2016-2017 period with a need to return to basics. It was time to contract and focus again. I could see how we could cut and become smaller, become leaner and more profitable. I could see how we could refocus on our core business while maintaining steady sales and profit. That part was straightforward. We put together a six-month plan, including offering early retirement to many of our core staff, drastically reducing our overhead and scope of business.

Part of the recognition was that, at least for the time being, we were going to produce significantly less top line, so we needed to cut our operating costs to reflect the size of the company we now projected to be. We needed to be an operation that reliably generated profit in this new reality. That part was relatively easy, even though downsizing decisions are always bittersweet.

Trimming fat, cutting overhead, focusing on our core business. All fairly straightforward. All with clear benefits that would allow us to be lean and mean. My tenure as CEO, however, was premised on the idea that I would lead.

We were a team. We had fought battles together. Many of the staff had bled for me and I had bled for them. In the past, every time I had gone in front of my team to say we needed to endure short-term suffering, I always had a vision for the next step. There was always a new goal, a way for us to ascend to the next step up.

This time, my vision and my confidence were failing me. I saw the need to find the next iteration of how we would enrich lifestyles by providing products and services to make everyday life more fulfilling. Our purpose still mattered. But how would we accomplish that in the digital era? What was the next version of Shop Jabranding?

I believe there's either progression or regression. Even in times when we had gone through periods of regression, I always had a clear image of what the next step was. Pain, for the purpose of moving forward, never bothered me. I envisioned how we could contract and be a solid, profitable company. I was concerned we might lose some relevance and our position as a leader, but more importantly I felt we had lost our courage to innovate and try new things.

We were no longer an independent company. We were part of a group, and expected to contribute our share of the revenue and profits to our holding company. A significant decline in revenue and profit was not acceptable. Where OLM and I had once been lauded for our performance, now every action was scrutinized and questioned.

I was the face of OLM. Fairly or not, I received the lion's share of the credit when things went well. Now, I was receiving the lion's share of the blame. I was too lenient. I was too risk-taking. I was too flamboyant. I had chosen the mantle of leadership, so it was my responsibility to take the blame.

The problem with innovation is that there must be latitude to fail as well as to succeed. With each successive year, the pressure to increase sales and profitability went up, while the tolerance for innovation went down. It became a stifling environment.

Our sense of purpose also came under fire. When things were going well, the idea of OLM as a purpose-driven company was embraced. As performance declined, the message to me changed. "Profit and performance are what matters," I was told, in no uncertain terms. "Think about purpose after profit. Get your priorities straight!" I have always believed that is a false dichotomy.

I was the CEO and I was given a mandate — to restore performance. I was confident we could achieve the performance objectives in the short term, but worried it would be at the expense of our culture. The culture we'd worked long and hard at shaping and nurturing. We would need to become a sort of organization that I didn't feel I could responsibly lead. I couldn't stand in front of my team to say that I had a plan for our next step, where all of our stakeholders benefited, because I didn't. For almost 20 years, the PCT Philosophy had guided us. We generated profit to benefit our stakeholders, and the hierarchy of importance was: customers, employees, business partners, society and, finally, shareholders.

Perhaps I was too late in facing up to the reality of being part of a large corporate conglomerate. Performance and profit must come first. Trying to realign my values to this new reality caused me to lose my own sense of purpose. Sacrificing employees and business partners to ensure short-term returns wasn't a clear enough purpose for me to stand, in good faith, in front of my team and represent.

Resolving too much overhead is easy. Boom, fixed.

Changing business environments? OK, that happens, and we have to constantly challenge ourselves to learn, adapt and seek new opportunities.

But the issue of failed new initiatives was a problem. Over an 18-month period we had several failed projects. From my fighting perspective, innovation is like throwing punches and kicks, probing for an opening and an opportunity. If we stop probing, we never find the opportunity. But it had been 18 months. A long time; too long. We were searching for how to compete in a changing environment, but not finding signs. From a fighter's perspective, we decided to move down through the divisions. To descend back down through the rankings. We'd go back to fighting in an easier arena. That was a completely reasonable business decision, but it was an existential question for me personally.

As the president and CEO, I felt that without change, without challenge, the best we could do was refocus and be 'good,' but gradually get smaller and less relevant. Honestly, making a decision that the best course of action is to focus on being smaller, but resilient and profitable, is a sound business plan. Helping OLM get to that stage of being leaner and more profitable was my responsibility. But making that our story going forward was not a plan I could lead in good faith. Every time I had gone to our employees to ask them to sacrifice, it was always with a clear sense of needing to cut back, and experience temporary suffering in order to achieve the next level of long-term gain. I had always believed in that, 100%. I would get buy-in from my team. But this time that was not the case.

I didn't see the next level, where the next potential for growth was. Clearly my shareholders and I had a very different vision for the company. I knew my responsibility.

I led the restructuring. I took all the blame for our failed projects. I took the blame for failing to meet the budget. I led the charge in cutting back, so that OLM was leaner and more profitable. If I couldn't provide a plan that I believed was true to our purpose for the next level of growth, my responsibility was to hand over the company in the best shape possible for the new management team. I took the fall, so hopefully the next team would not be burdened by the need to make hard decisions at the start. That was the best service I could see that I could provide to OLM at that time.

Many times, my staff had asked me, "What do I need to do to become CEO?" My reply was always the same: "The person with the biggest, clearest vision of how we move forward is the best person to do this job. If you have a bigger, clearer vision than me, then I should cede to you. Until you do, follow me."

I no longer had the biggest, clearest vision. It was time for me to go.

And so, after we'd completed the most traumatic stage of our restructuring, I stepped down as CEO in September of 2017.

LOOKING FOR SOMETHING NEW

POST-SHOP JAPAN

I was confronted with an existential problem. Who am I?

For the last six months of my tenure at OLM, I had significant trouble sleeping. I would wake up at 2 or 3 in the morning, my mind racing through what I should do. The actions I needed to get OLM back to profitability were clear. It would entail pain and sacrifice. I had taken similar actions before, but without a clear vision, and without the support of my board and shareholders, it became clear that I'd reached the end of the road.

Once I realized that I needed to leave the company, my concerns about lack of clarity turned to myself. After so many years of internalizing and embracing my role as representative director of Oak Lawn Marketing, who was Harry Hill when I no longer held that role?

In my search for the answer, I had to confront three things:

1. Who am I really?
2. How do I come to terms with not having a salary? What does wealth mean to me?
3. Have I gotten old? Or, perhaps, the question was how do I stay young? Had I lost my will to fight?

WHO AM I REALLY?

I suspect that anyone who has been successful and ends a chapter in their life faces this question.

In Japan, we are often referred to by our title. After 12 years as the CEO (in Japanese, the *Shacho*), that is how I had come to define myself.

I was no longer the *Shacho*. Does the title make the person, or does the person define the title? That was an existential problem.

People didn't stand up anymore when I walked in the room. I wasn't the center of attention. My personal assistant didn't perfectly time delivering my coffee when I arrived at my desk. Without the trappings of power and influence, who am I? Do the people around me still care? Was I diminished in the eyes of my family, the people in my company, in the industry, my network, trade associations ... all the people who identified me as the CEO of OLM? If I'm not the guy who wields that power, am I no longer the person I'd been? Do I no longer count in the world?

For me personally, this was important because Shop Japan and Oak Lawn Marketing stood for many things.

We were principled, passionate, innovative and inspiring. As I came to grips with my post-OLM self, I realized that those concepts are in fact me.

Thankfully, it became clear that the majority of the people around me afforded me the same level of respect. My accomplishments and legacy hadn't changed. As just Harry Hill, the American Chamber of Commerce in Japan still elected me to sit on its board. I was still considered one of the leaders. I was still relevant. The chamber even asked me to run for president after I'd stepped down as CEO. Actually, for some people, my not being CEO seemed to make it easier to ask me for favors and for me to donate my time.

So, one of the things that was really important in finding myself was realizing that I had standing and influence in the world regardless of my title, because of who I am, and what I had achieved. After 20 years in the company and 12 years with the title, I realized that I had started to identify myself so much with that honorific that I'd forgotten who I was. So, it was an important process to go through. It was traumatic — a trauma that many people have when faced with a post-career change of life — but I slowly became comfortable with my post OLM CEO-self. Now, I needed to find my next purpose.

NO LONGER HAVING A SALARY

The second crisis I went through was suddenly no longer receiving a monthly salary.

My goal in terms of wealth accumulation has always been for my money to make more money than I do. And as soon as my money was making more than I did, I would no longer be dependent on working to survive and to support my family.

Over the years, I got to the point where I was making a significant amount of money on an annual basis. So, for my money to make more money than I did, I had to accumulate more wealth and to invest wisely.

I had met a woman in the early 2000s, as I was starting to realize more financial success, who became my financial advisor. Over the course of 20 years or so, she had created a very successful wealth management company with offices in Hong Kong, Tokyo and New York. From the beginning, I told her that my goal was to create wealth for her to manage with a moderate to low risk profile. I was constantly betting on myself — which I considered high-risk, because something could always happen to me — so I wanted the money she managed to be independent of me. To that end, for more than 15 years I contributed to the pot without really withdrawing.

When I stepped down as the head of Shop Japan, I had wealth and assets. Nevertheless, it was a shock when, suddenly, the monthly salary stopped rolling in.

Many people struggle when their monthly salary becomes an anchor. It's one of the ways, without even thinking about it, people define themselves. And when it's gone, there can be trauma.

And so, I had to embrace the fact that I had, in fact, achieved my goal: my assets were making more money than I had been generating through my salary. I found a new freedom in not being beholden to or dependent on working at a particular company for a fixed income. My financial advisor and her firm had done their job. My assets could generate income for my family and me to live on, quite nicely, without depleting them. They were still growing, I could live comfortably, I could try new things.

I was able to deal with this second transition.

HOW TO STAY YOUNG

At Shop Japan/OLM, we talked about PTW, Passion to Wow. Passion and purpose made it easy for me to get up every day. I always had something to fight for. It focused my energy and made me a better leader. At an ACCJ presentation, I heard Barry Eisler, author of the John Rain series of thrillers, explain how to become a writer: "Indulge your passions." Ever since hearing that turn of phrase, I have incorporated it into my lexicon. At Shop Japan, we had a passion for providing value to our customers through fitness, sleep, nutrition, cleaning, cooking and hearing, with all the products and services we sold. We had many passions, because without passion for each and every area of our business, we wouldn't be able to 'wow' our customers.

Immediately after stepping down from OLM, two things happened. I gained a lot of weight, even though I was still working out regularly. And, for lack of a better term, I got old. My posture became slightly hunched. I was only 55, but I felt like I had lost my vim and vigor. I am a firm believer in wisdom, the knowledge that accumulates by learning from experience. I embraced the notion of age bringing wisdom, but I was not ready to be downright old.

What did I need to stay young? Passion and purpose. I needed to identify my passions and pursue them, indulge them. There's an important difference between being controlled by your passions — which turns into lust or addiction or any number of obsessions or dependencies that can lead people astray — and indulging your passions. When I indulge my passions, I am in control. When I am controlled by my passions, I lose myself.

Why had I lost my passion? Because I didn't have anything that was inspiring me, making me excited to wake up in the morning. I didn't have a purpose.

I asked myself what the passions were that would drive me to the next stage of my life. I identified four recurring themes: family, education, fitness and martial arts, and the direct-to-consumer business.

FAMILY

The first two passions I identified were family and education, areas where I felt I had credibility and could make a difference.

First, I felt I could make a difference by giving opportunities to my family and the important people around me. I'd always felt that OLM was an extended family. Our PCT Philosophy was about caring and empowering. I decided that I would not focus solely on myself, but re-focus on karma, in a sense. I always believed that karma is enlightened self-interest. Almost inevitably, when I focused on providing opportunities for others, I gained as much or greater benefit for myself. I was not so much a believer in altruism as I was in creating a bigger pie. As an adherent to the expanding pie theory, I knew that if we created a larger pool of rewards, I would also reap the benefits. My family and close network are my legacy, so first and foremost I wanted to help them create.

I also felt my philosophy on how to raise a family (similar to my ideology of leadership and running a company) had a deeper, more relevant meaning for society, particularly Japanese society. I feel there is a crisis in the fundamental family unit. I suspect it may not just be in Japan.

I am shocked by how many people around me feel that the opportunities today are fewer than those of yesterday. Although I had come from a challenging childhood environment, often without much money, my parents (all four of them) always nourished my mind and my capacity to dream. In addition, they encouraged and supported my actions to turn those dreams into reality. Dreams without action are just dreams. Dreams coupled with action unlock new possibilities, often different from the original goal.

This last point, I believe, is the most important value I try to instil in my children and the people around me. Building an action plan around pursuing a dream requires the next level of imagination. Turning a dream into purpose. Creating purpose activates the fight instinct and creates a hunger. It requires discipline, passion and dedication.

When my children were young, I allowed them to pursue any activity they wished. My only requirement was that they loved doing it and they tried their best. Otherwise, I would stop supporting it. Three of my kids ended up getting basketball scholarships in the US — two of them at Division 1 schools. The other two got partial academic scholarships, after excelling at baseball and soccer in high school. I'm proud that in the pursuit of excellence and following their passions, they learned to succeed in multiple facets of life. They learned how to dream and pursue their dreams. That's a skill that is evergreen. One stage of your life may end, but if we know the process of building success, it can be recreated. That's quite different from building a single perishable skill.

When I shared this philosophy of following your dream, the parents of my children's peers would say, "Your children can have dreams, but mine can't because they are not your children, coming from such privilege. They just don't have the same opportunities."

The worst thing you can do to a child, particularly as a parent, is to put a ceiling over them. Childhood and early adulthood are about discovery. Finding what you excel at, what you love. Revel in learning the process of repeated excellence and success. What I see too often is over-specialization in study, athletics and interests. Curiosity is replaced with a rush to specialize. David Epstein's book *Range: How Generalists Triumph in a Specialized World* provides a scientific analysis of what was Yumiko's and my approach to raising our kids. Giving them the opportunity and confidence to be curious and to experiment gave them the best opportunities for future growth.

Over-specialization can particularly go awry with athletes, when they don't apply the rigor and discipline with which they approach their sports to their everyday life. Success on the court or the ball field requires passion, hard work and a certain amount of luck. The number of people who can make a living as an athlete is quite small. It is essentially a lottery. A gene pool lottery and a lottery to avoid major injury. Athletes can do everything right, suffer a catastrophic injury, and their career is over. I watched so many of my children's peers peak in high school and have little to fall back on. Like the Bruce Springsteen song *Glory Days*, about a couple who had their best years in high school and reminisced rather than moving forward.

For me, family is a unit that enables and empowers the individuals within, very similar to a well-run corporation, but different in that the support and love I gave my children is forever. Yumiko's and my role as parents is to empower and enable our children to learn the process of finding something they can succeed at and that makes them happy. Not what we approve of, or makes us happy, but what makes them happy and successful.

In Japan, my generation of parents came of age as the post-war economic bubble came to an end. This generation of Japanese in many ways are more conservative and risk averse than their parents and their parents' parents, even though there's more stability and excess today than when their parents and grandparents grew up.

My experience is that the less hardship and toil people experience, the more fearful they become. By not giving our children the opportunity to experiment and fail, we make them less able to cope with life. As I said, I never hire anyone who has not experienced and overcome some degree of failure. As parents, letting kids experiment and learn how to succeed (or overcome failure) is the most important life lesson we can give. Not a specialized skill, but the skill to create specialties throughout life. I learned by fighting on the playground. I believe all of us, particularly children, need to learn this skill in our own way. We have to find an equivalent environment to fighting on the playground to teach our children how to deal with adversity.

This is a philosophy I believe in deeply. It was transformative in my life. I believe it has been transformative in my children's lives.

I felt that the next step in my life was not only to find ways that I could support my own immediate family but also my immediate circle of influence, the people I cared about. So, I began to muse over the question, "How do I inspire them? How do I get them to follow, believe and build on their dreams?"

I learned a valuable lesson from my parents about pursuing passion, optimism and dreams. I had built a successful management philosophy on the tenets of this lesson. We can't make our children succeed, but we can make it easier for them to fail. Just like in business, as the leaders of our families, we must create an environment that fosters growth and sustained success.

I knew I had found one important theme: family.

EDUCATION

My second post-retirement theme was education. In 2014 the White House department of personnel appointed me co-chair of CULCON, the US-Japan Conference on Cultural and Educational Interchange. This bilateral commission promotes public and private partnerships, and advises both governments on identifying and nurturing the next generation of Japan-US leaders. CULCON was started by President Kennedy and Prime Minister Ikeda in 1962, with the premise that true friendship between nations is fostered by building long-term, grassroots connections.

During my tenure at CULCON, one of the major themes was to increase the number of exchange students studying for a semester or more in both directions. The number of Japanese students studying in the US had fallen from more than 30,000 to about 12,000 annually, a roughly 70% drop. The number of US students in Japan had increased, to about 8,000 a year, but the overall traffic was down.

In the early 1990s, Congressmen were smashing Toshiba tape recorders on the steps of the US Capitol. Japan was considered more of a threat than an ally.

By 2014, there was no question that Japan was seen first and foremost as an ally. In all areas — education, government and the private sector — long-term friendships made it easier for people on both sides of the Pacific to work together, and to resolve problems when they arose. With the dramatic decrease in the number of students traveling between the US and Japan, we in CULCON worried about how that relationship would fare 20-30 years in the future.

I initially came to Japan as an English teacher. I have tremendous gratitude to the Japanese government for creating the JET (Japan English Teaching) Program, which first brought me there. As a cultural exchange initiative, I believe JET has been extraordinarily successful in creating Japan experts, not only among Americans, but throughout the world. It has created a network of constituents who are friends of Japan, and often lead cross-cultural initiatives in the public and private sectors. JET has been a success, except ironically with the one thing it says it's supposed to be doing: improving English-language education. As far as I can tell, English education in Japan has not improved at all over the decades I've been here. A newspaper article in 2023 reported that Japanese high school students ranked below Cambodia on standardized English tests.

Having lived in Japan for more than 30 years, I know this is not because of some inherent language learning deficiency in the Japanese people. Instead, it's the teaching system that is broken. Language learning pedagogy shows that active learning coupled with physical movement is the most effective method of acquiring language skills. Yet, Japan still focuses on the teacher speaking and the student listening. This is the least effective way to teach language. Doing more of it hasn't changed the harsh reality of how Japanese students perform on international standardized English tests, and continuing the same approach never will.

The tourism industry in Japan is booming. The Japanese population is decreasing, so domestic companies looking to expand need to look outside the country. English education responds to both of these needs and opportunities. Still, the approach isn't changing. Like my focus on family, this is a theme that I believe I understand and can positively influence.

I also believe it's incumbent on people of my generation to inspire and provide opportunity for young people. I often speak to business groups, and a recurring comment I hear from my generation of leaders is, "Japanese people today don't have the same courage and curiosity that our generation had when we were young." My answer is always the same: "If what you say is true, that young people don't have the same courage and the same dreams, it's not a problem with the young people. The problem is with us, because we haven't provided that inspiration." As with family, I feel I have an important message to share on that.

The problem with Japanese education, I think, goes deeper. Particularly in Japanese high schools, the focus on specialization goes to unhealthy extremes. For the academically focused, the sole aim becomes getting ready for the college entrance examination. This involves a lot of rote learning. For athletes, coaches focus on competition to the exclusion of all else, including the players' safety. The high school years should be a time for young people to learn the skills that will serve them for the rest of their lives. In Japan, unfortunately, they're learning skills that will serve them in the immediate future, often with little or no thought given to developing long-term skills. What an abdication of responsibility! And I see this focus on over-specialization happening in the US and other developed countries as well.

A family structure that too often places an unnecessary, self-imposed ceiling over young people's heads.

An education system, particularly post-junior high school, that focuses on short-term results rather than skills for the future. How unfortunate. In a rapidly changing world, perhaps the most important skill is how to learn, unlearn and learn again. In business we call it learning how to pivot. When my peers complain that today's young person is not equipped with the skills to compete in today's world, they need look no further than the mirror for the cause of this dilemma.

FITNESS AND MARTIAL ARTS

My third theme as I moved forward in my life was martial arts and fitness. In many ways, Shop Japan created the home fitness industry in Japan. At the very least we had a huge impact in helping to create a fitness culture among people of all ages, where they can participate both inside and outside of their homes. We sold iconic products that became hits in almost every demographic. People still talk about those products today.

I came to Japan because of martial arts. Fighting had been a part of my life from an early age. Shorinji Kempo taught me how to focus this skill beyond winning and losing. Balancing body and mind became my way of life. A strong mind needs a strong body, and vice versa. I lived my life this way, and Shop Japan became extremely successful in giving our customers the tools to pursue a healthy lifestyle.

At the age of 42, I started kickboxing. I had never been in the ring, and I wanted that experience. Fighting in some form has shaped my life. Learning to fight gave me confidence, and the resilience to get up if I'd been knocked down. Staying in shape made me feel good about myself.

Staying in shape is a commitment to oneself. It's a habit that can be acquired. We're surrounded by pills and supplements, but sustained exercise is the most effective way to maintain health. If we could turn the benefits of sustained exercise into a pill, everyone would buy it. Motivating and inspiring people to exercise for health and performance was my third next-stage theme.

CUSTOMER-FACING

My final passion, as I moved into this phase in my life, was to focus on customer-facing, or direct-to-consumer, businesses. I was asked to interview for several positions as the country manager for business-to-business (B2B) type companies. While I felt I could potentially do the jobs, none of the opportunities excited me. As I thought about what made me passionate, I realized it was making a direct difference in people's lives.

As I had come to grips with the fact that I didn't need to work, from a financial standpoint, I was afforded the luxury of focusing on what I truly wanted to do. I wanted my next venture or passion projects to touch on one or more of these four themes.

Two years after stepping down as CEO of OLM/Shop Japan, I founded Better-U. Our vision is that fitness and education are lifelong endeavors. It's never too late to create a better version of yourself, to 'version me up.'

Our first line of business was to be the master franchise partner in Japan for UFC Gym, which has fitness centers in 33 countries and is a subsidiary of the UFC, one of the biggest sports promotion brands in the world. Because our purpose was fitness and education, I knew that I had to be the first person to walk the talk. Looking at myself in the mirror, I had become fat and old, so getting back in shape became a mandate.

Better-U came about from a dinner conversation with my good friend, Eiji Tezuka, the master franchise owner and CEO of Gold's Gym in Japan. His company had secured the Japanese rights to the UFC Gym franchise, and he asked if I wanted to joint venture this opportunity with him.

My first-blush impression was that UFC Gym was strictly a fight club. After all, it takes its name from the Ultimate Fighting Championship, a mixed martial arts program. As much as I enjoy fighting, it didn't sound like a scalable business. So, my reaction was 'no.' Out of respect for Eiji, though, I agreed to research UFC Gym, and visited some of their locations in California. I studied their culture. Their vision is to 'train different.' UFC athletes are some of the best-conditioned athletes in the world. They need to be proficient in multiple disciplines, as well as have strength, flexibility and endurance. The UFC Gym is a place where the everyday person can train like a UFC athlete. This vision was very similar to my philosophy of learning. It was more in line with the training process of the generalist than the specialist. I came to see that I could believe in this vision.

The mission of the UFC Gym is empowering the fighting spirit, embodied in the phrase 'What's your fight?' My mission for most of the previous 20 years had been to help the everyday person overcome their personal complexes, to live a more fulfilled life. And so, enriching people's lifestyle became 'What's your fight?' But my purpose, giving people the skills to live healthier and happier, remained the same.

The UFC Gym also gave me an opportunity to create an international environment. In America, it aspires to be the most family-friendly gym in the country. In Japan, we too focus on family and fitness. Our market research informed us that this was a message that the market would respond to. For our junior members, we have also created an English learning system. We have incorporated language acquisition through total physical response (tpr), the most efficient way for people, particularly children, to learn a language.

I was neither looking for nor expecting to find a single business that met all of the four passions I had identified, but as we developed the business plan for Better-U and the expansion of the UFC Gym in Japan, it checked all the boxes. It seemed the obvious next step.

I had found a new purpose. Better-U was established in April of 2019, a year and a half after I had stepped down as CEO from Oak Lawn Marketing.

CRISIS TO CRISIS

Once again, I was starting from scratch. After leading a large organization for so many years, I had to relearn the skills of a start-up, and endure the rigors of bootstrapping. Creating something from nothing takes work. And so, 2019 was spent preparing, looking for a first location and hiring people. Starting from square one is difficult. Little did I know how difficult it would be.

In December of 2019, we identified our first location for the UFC Gym Japan. We were able to take over a failed yoga studio. With gyms, the largest initial investment is usually around environmental control and locker rooms, but we would be able to use the existing infrastructure with a relatively modest upfront investment.

It seemed like the world was lining up in our favor. We had done our market research. Our first location was in an affluent residential area of Tokyo, an area with lots of families. We would create an international environment, offering small group classes so we could focus on premium, personalized service. We were confident we could provide a great synergy between Japanese and foreign cultures.

We were hoping to recreate the energy of the gyms I'd seen in the US, where families could train at the same facility, while helping members acquire functional English.

Our research showed that a medium-size gym focusing on performance training, with an international flavor, filled a need. We got ready. We embarked on an aggressive but achievable 90-day refurbishment of the facility. We kept costs within budget. We started construction in January, 2020, with plans to open three months later. We had a successful membership pre-sale, and things were looking good all around.

What could go wrong?

THE WORLD
FALLS APART

We officially opened on 6 April, 2020. The COVID-19 emergency declaration in Japan was announced on 9 April, and we closed our doors on 10 April. We had been open for all of three days! Sixty days later, we were able to reopen the doors. Of the 150 people who had signed up as part of the pre-sale promotion, fewer than 40 ever set foot in the gym.

Nothing went according to plan. Keeping members was difficult. Finding staff was even harder. Marketing and selling were almost impossible, because throughout the protracted COVID-19 crisis, the government appeared to be discouraging the use of gyms. We had myriad health and safety rules: masks, social distancing, disinfecting and so on.

Inside the gym, members didn't know how to act. Our business concept was built around being fun, outgoing and friendly. Under the weight of the pandemic, we had to largely muzzle our personality.

Not for the first time, I had a business with no roadmap. With the world in flux, long-range planning was impossible. We focused on surviving.

Although we had fewer than 200 members, they depended upon us to keep the doors open. We were a refuge, a place to recharge. One of our members dubbed us the 'third place,' after home and work. In a world of uncertainty, with no real means to grow, we focused on providing the best possible environment for the members, coaches and staff who persevered.

It was hard. Members would get sick and quit. Same with our employees. Those members who have been with us from the beginning appreciated that we were committed to staying open and operating in the safest way possible. By hook or by crook, that's what we did.

As always, I espoused the two Ps: purpose and profit. For our first couple of years, profit was inconceivable. There was no real way to make money, but then almost nobody in the fitness industry was making money. So, we had to either give up entirely, or try to focus on purpose and survival until the world settled down.

Circumstances changed rapidly. Uncertainty was pervasive. Our employees felt stressed all the time. While the Japanese government never resorted to passing laws requiring people to stay home or wear masks, it recommended that they do so. Coming to the gym, even while wearing a mask, appeared to be a gray area. In the US and many other parts of the world, a recommendation without a means to enforce it is often ignored. In Japan, the recommendation, the social rule, became paramount. Our purpose appeared to be at odds with the recommendation of the government. This put tremendous stress on us, particularly our Japanese staff.

But we persevered. We gained loyal members. We managed to get by. After re-opening in June of 2020, we never closed our doors again. In February of 2022, good news appeared to be on the horizon. The government was indicating that it would lift the Limited State of Emergency in April.

We now had two gyms in Tokyo, but February 2022 was our most difficult month. More than 50% of our staff and coaches either had COVID-19 or were in quarantine because somebody in their family had tested positive for the virus. My son Ken and I were opening and closing our two locations every day, starting at 6 in the morning and finishing at 11 at night. We had pledged to stay true to our purpose to provide the third place.

On 23 February, 2022, almost all of our employees were due to return to work. We would be back to full strength. It was a Tuesday morning. I was sitting in our original location, welcoming back my team. It felt to me like I could finally let myself believe that the worst of the pandemic was over. The Limited State of Emergency would be lifted in less than six weeks. We could finally start planning for the future like a real business.

It was at that precise time that some mischievous god decided to throw a new obstacle at us.

Our original gym location, in a suburban neighborhood of Tokyo, is in the basement of a small building. At the bottom of the stairs is a square foyer. The walls surrounding the open-air foyer are glass, so it is essentially an outdoor enclosure in the middle of our gym. We had set up tables and chairs in this area. From the perspective of welcoming prospective members, they would walk down the stairs and immediately feel like they were in the middle of the gym. Particularly in the spring and fall, it was very comfortable to sit outside and work.

On that Tuesday morning, I was sitting at a corner table in the lobby, sipping coffee and working on my computer, when I became aware of a crowd of people in the foyer area. As I walked over to see what was going on, a man in a uniform walked in the front door holding a badge aloft demanding to know who was in charge. I replied that I was. He brusquely told me to follow him. I stepped outside into the foyer and saw my general manager surrounded by policemen. They sat me down next to him. He had been in COVID-19 quarantine, so I hadn't seen him in three weeks. They read him an arrest warrant for the importing of 大麻 (*taima*), the Japanese word for cannabis. To me they read a search warrant for the premises.

We had 30 members in the gym, participating in classes. Everybody could see there was a commotion in the foyer, but they weren't aware of what was happening. The police informed me that nobody was allowed to go in or out as they searched the premises for the next several hours.

This was a new unanticipated crisis.

Now I can laugh that I ticked two things off my bucket list, although they certainly weren't actually on any sort of wish list. I had a search warrant presented to me, and I was subsequently interrogated by the police for close to seven hours.

Although this was a first for me, I called on my experience watching US police dramas on TV to help navigate the process. I quickly discovered that this knowledge would not help me.

As the police started to search the gym, I hit the speed dial on my phone to call my personal attorney and good friend, John Sasaki. Mid-sentence, as I tried to tell him what was going on, the police confiscated my phone. It seems we were not allowed to make any calls as they were searching the premises.

Later, when I went to the police station to be questioned, I told them I wanted to be accompanied by an attorney. Once again, they said 'no.' After taking my statement, the police produced a document for me to sign. After I signed, I asked for a copy. Once again, 'no.'

As unsettling as all of this was, I remained calm. I knew I had nothing to hide, that I was not guilty of committing a crime. I also knew that, sometimes, not being guilty is not enough, so, of course, there was risk. John was on standby during my questioning. We agreed that if he didn't hear from me by a certain time, he would have to assume I was in custody and take action to defend me. This was a new problem, a new challenge. Knowing that I had overcome all manner of challenges before enabled me to distance myself and keep perspective.

When I coach my kickboxing conditioning classes, I often start the session with a question. How does this differ from other types of physical conditioning, such as training for a marathon? I explain that the goal for marathon conditioning is to train to complete 42 kilometers as fast as possible. It requires a specific type of training and focus. The goal of kickboxing conditioning is to be able to complete five three-minute rounds with a one-minute rest interval. The conditioning requires technique, endurance and interval bursts. Inevitably, the heart rate will spike. How to continue to focus and perform even when one's heart is beating full-speed, and how to recover quickly, is an integral part of the training. The conditioning essentially simulates the stress situation of the ring. In the world of *budo*, Japanese martial arts, maintaining the ability to think clearly even under duress is the concept of *heijo-shin*, or calm heart.

Staying calm, having the world slow down internally, even as it is speeding up on the outside, has benefited me in all areas of my life. The training I've done in the ring or a fenced martial arts cage has certainly paid dividends at the negotiating table or in the boardroom. It paid dividends as I was being questioned by the police. My interrogator repeated my answer after each question as he typed my replies into the computer. Every third or fourth question, his restatement of my reply was wildly inaccurate. After this happened a few times, I realized that this was simply a technique to test me. To see if I would be consistent in my replies. Now here was something I'd learned on the American cop shows after all. Like watching an opponent through feints and jabs, once I understood what they were doing, it was easier to respond.

I talked with John and introduced my general manager and his wife to a well recommended defense attorney. Once I made sure that he had good counsel, I felt I had completed my obligation to him. I had to focus on ensuring the well-being of Better-U and the UFC Gym Japan. I also found legal representation for the gym in the event that we needed it.

Japan can be an unforgiving place, particularly on issues involving illegal drugs. Even if we were subsequently found to have done nothing wrong, just being in the news, simply being associated with all the negative publicity, could cause a loss of trust and business. We had survived COVID-19, but once again we were fighting for our life.

We did what I have always thought is the right thing to do when a crisis happens. We were honest, transparent and communicative.

On the evening that my general manager was escorted from the gym in handcuffs and ankle chains, I sent out a message to every one of our members, telling them exactly what had happened. Both of our gym locations were searched. Our general manager was arrested. Those were the facts. I apologized for the inconvenience we had caused. The accused was well liked, and on behalf of the staff and the members, I expressed the hope that he and his family would be OK. But our purpose was unchanged. We needed to be the 'third place' for our members.

We didn't lose one member.

They appreciated our honesty and transparency. We treated them with respect and trust, and they returned that trust. I think they implicitly understood that it would have been easy to give up. We'd sacrificed our time and our money to stay open, to be there for them, through the toughest of times. Our members appreciated that, and they now gave us the benefit of the doubt. At least for the time being.

We embraced the responsibility of being their third place. When this crisis hit, we dealt with it head on. We didn't hide or sugar-coat it. We didn't say any more or any less than exactly what we knew. I had done this type of communication. I had the experience of the True Sleeper incident, and countless other bumps in the road, to draw on. Communicate. Treat customers with respect and trust.

As I've said repeatedly here, I believe in transparency. If you can't trust the people around you — if you can't put your faith in your customers, your employees, your colleagues, your business partners — then you're in the wrong business. We had built that level of trust.

We communicated. People were shocked. They talked about it. We survived the initial shock.

The gym had been underperforming for several months. We'd lost key staff. I had rationalized that the problems were due to the continued stress of COVID-19, which was certainly true, but now I think there were probably other issues at work that I had missed. We had a great core team of coaches, but we needed to recreate a management team and support staff almost from zero.

Once again, I was confronted with a need to reboot. Once again, I needed to clean house and start fresh. I'd been in this situation before. And reboots, while painful, have usually brought benefits. Ironically, this time, the cleansing process was actually easier than in the past. I didn't have to layoff the old management team, which usually takes time and causes trauma. The old management team was simply gone. On 24 February, we started anew.

Various people stepped up, including my son Ken, my daughters Ellie and Mari, and Ellie's husband, Ed. Ken assumed the critical management and operations role. All this time, I had espoused my values and role as empowering and providing opportunity for my family. Now, not for the first time, the shoe was on the other foot. My family saved me. And I don't mean that in a metaphorical way. They literally stepped into the breach and saved me; saved the business.

February 2022 turned out to be our darkest month. We slogged through it. By the end of March, we had a new and motivated management team and the worst of COVID-19 was over. We were finally poised to grow and succeed.

I was reminded of three important life lessons.

First: When in doubt, keep moving forward, don't stop. In a fight, if you stop moving, if you stop probing, you never find an opportunity. When in doubt, never stop taking action. But all actions must have intent.

Second: What doesn't kill you makes you stronger. I've always said that the only mistake that I can't forgive is death, because nobody comes back from the dead. And in our situation, we had a lot of things that came close to killing us, but everything eventually made us stronger. In a fight, keep your guard up. I've been on the mat, but somehow or another I've always gotten back up.

Third: You've got to believe in your team. If you've got the right people on board and can believe in your team, you'll find a way out. Sometimes you have to change the team. Sometimes you have to switch teams. The ability to pivot is just as important as the ability to create a plan. While being a fighter seems like a one-person effort, great fighters have built a team around them, to put them in a position to win. As CEO of OLM, I got the credit when we excelled, but it was down to the effort and results of the team. As of February of 2022, I hadn't built a winning team. Then the best possible thing happened — we put a new team in place. The right people stepped up. Since those dark days, our first two gyms have seen steady growth, and we opened our third location in 2023.

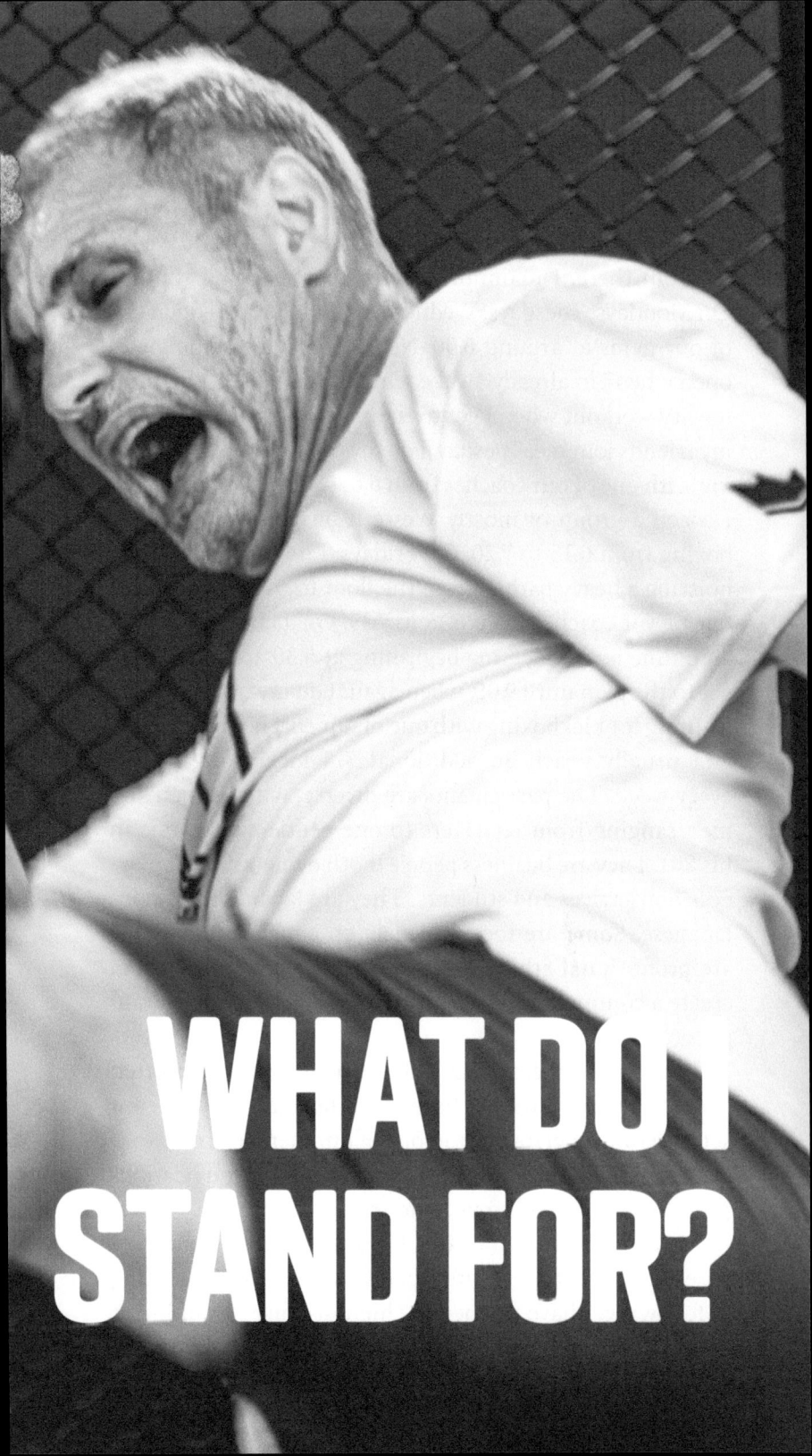

WHAT DO I STAND FOR?

Most days I wake up between 4 and 4.30 am. I check and respond to email. Over my first cup of coffee, I have a look at the news, my schedule and priorities for the day and week.

From there, I maintain a consistent morning routine. On Mondays, Tuesdays, Wednesdays and Fridays I open one of our gyms at around 6.00. No sense paying someone to open when I'm already awake. On Mondays, I do a high-intensity workout when I get to the gym. Sometimes a few of my friends join me. Tuesday, I do my own kickboxing training with one of our coaches from 6 to 7.30. On Wednesdays, I coach a group of mostly Western businessmen in kickboxing from 6.15 to 7.20. On Fridays, I do Olympic lifts — hoisting a heavy barbell from the floor to overhead — with one of our coaches from 6.15 to 7.35. On Thursdays, I have an online board meeting beginning at 5.30 am and I don't get to the gym until 9.00, when again I do my own personal training for kickboxing with one of our coaches in the cage.

I usually coach an additional 3-4 kickboxing classes every week. The participants are diverse, with women and men ranging from teenagers to one gentleman who is in his 80s. They are business people (both owners and employees), housewives and students. They are Japanese and non-Japanese. Some are focused solely on conditioning. Some are professional athletes. All of us have come together to create a community. We are different, but we share certain passions and values.

In addition to coaching kickboxing, my members often come to me for advice. I have given business advice, even acting as an angel investor in one of our member's new ventures. I have given career advice, family advice and relationship advice. I have become a life coach.

In the introduction to this book, I introduced the Purpose Spectrum. In the course of my career, whether leading or following, I have reached my highest sense of fulfilment both professionally and personally when I have been driven by purpose. You've heard me come back to that theme throughout these pages. This has helped me achieve the greatest rewards, including financial.

Purpose and profit have never been a trade-off. I believe that's a false equivalency. In my career, I have met very few people who were driven solely by money. Almost all of them ultimately find that money alone is not enough, and sooner or later experience the need to search for a purpose. My strong belief is that we all should search for a deep sense of purpose sooner rather than later.

As a leader, money was never the best way to motivate. Yes, it is important and provides incentive. But once a bonus is paid, it no longer motivates. Purpose, on the other hand, drives meaning and motivation every day.

Another theme of this book has been fighting. Knowing how to fight, learning how to stay calm in the most stressful situations, learning how not to lose. I fight. I fight for a purpose.

During my life, I have never been the smartest, the strongest or the richest. Yet, I have always found a way to lead. To inspire. To compete. I've found a way to succeed.

I had imagination that created dreams that created purpose that created a plan and drove me and others to action. I had discipline and optimism. I had my low points. I had a few enemies. When I was knocked down, I got up. I never gave up.

I have made a difference in the life of my family, in leading businesses, and in society. I started from humble and challenging beginnings. I have walked with the heavyweights. I have made a lot of money. I could have made more. Money is not a purpose. But purpose can make money.

What can you learn from me? I have achieved many special things, some of them great. But I truly believe that

I am not any more special than you. Follow your dreams, indulge your passions. Develop meaningful routines and habits. Stay disciplined but have fun. That is my message.

As noted, on most days, I wake up early. Usually, I get up with a spring in my step, ready to go. But I'm human, sometimes I feel a little tired. I feel like staying in bed and just lying around. But I serve a purpose, regardless of how I feel on any given day. I train; it's in my schedule, part of my routine. People will be waiting at the door of the gym if I don't get there on time. Even when I don't feel well, I always feel better following my workout. Staying true to my routine keeps me going. It keeps me young and keeps me relevant.

As I write these closing pages, I realize that the fight was never just about the victories in the cage or the triumphs in the boardroom. It was about the relentless pursuit of becoming a better man, husband, father, businessman, partner and martial artist. The journey wasn't just a phys-ical one — it was a soul-altering experience that shaped the very core of who I am. In every bruise, every challenge and every hard-fought moment, I found the true meaning of resilience. *Fighter!* is not just a memoir; it's a testament to the indomitable spirit within all of us. The battles may change, but the fight remains eternal.

So here I stand, not just as a fighter but as a living testament to the power of determination, discipline and the unyielding will to keep pushing forward. I invite you to reflect on your own fights, victories and the strength within. This is not just my story, it's an ode to the warrior within each of us.

Thank you for joining me on this journey. As you close this book, remember: the fight never truly ends. It merely transforms into the next chapter of your epic saga. Embrace it, conquer it, and let the echoes of your battle cry resonate through the arenas of your life. This is the end of one chapter, but the beginning of countless others. The fight lives on.

It takes tremendous courage to walk into the ring, any ring. An athlete fights to beat the opponent. The fight that you and I fight is for a meaningful life. Fighting is a metaphor and a skill to make us better human beings.

Even in the winter, when it is still dark and cold outside, I'm out the door and opening the gym at 6.00. This is my new purpose. I am a life coach. This book is my virtual gym for you.

On most days, I ride my bicycle to the gym. Sometimes, I drive my Ferrari.

EPILOGUE

Hayato Fujita Jr. first booked my Tuesday afternoon kickboxing conditioning class in April of 2022. I always check on who is attending the class before it begins. He had just joined the gym and my class was the first one he would attend.

I had a look at the notes in our system. He was 35 years old. It didn't say if he had any combat arts experience, but then I looked at his email address. It ended with @crazybee. gym.co.jp, the gym of Kid Yamamoto, one of the greatest Mixed Martial Arts fighters in the history of Japan. Now I knew he had experience, and I knew he had trained at a top gym. I had to be at my best.

He participated in my conditioning class. He was clearly experienced, but out of practice. He looked to be muscular and in good physical shape, but quickly became winded. His punches and kicks were technically excellent, but clearly not at their peak.

After class I introduced myself. Over the next several weeks and months, I got to know him. He was an ex-professional wrestler and champion from the Michinoku Pro Wrestling Federation. Five years earlier, he had been diagnosed with a rare form of skeletal cancer in the base of his spine. He had gone through numerous chemotherapy treatments and surgery. At one point, he was confined to a wheelchair, and it was not certain he would walk again.

Hayato is a fighter. He set up a mini gym in his hospital room to work out his upper body while fighting his cancer and rehabbing his lower body. After five long years, his doctors proclaimed him cancer-free. He came to our gym to begin the process of returning to form, to get back in the ring.

Over the next several months, Hayato's grit and determination were an inspiration to all who came into contact with him. While he also worked out at a professional fighting gym, he became a regular in my Tuesday and Wednesday afternoon classes, alongside housewives and businessmen. He told me that he came to my class for two reasons: to be able to train on his own, without the pressure of a professional fighting gym, and to remind himself that martial arts are fun.

In July of 2022, three months after re-starting serious training, he regained the Michinoku Championship Belt. Over the course of the next year and a half, he would defend the title numerous times and compete in several large crossover events with other organizations. His story was a true inspiration to all of us.

In December of 2023, Hayato learned that his cancer had reappeared. As of this writing, he is recovering from surgery.

Prior to this latest operation, he shared with us that he hoped to get back to the gym as soon as possible. However, he suspects that he will be confined to a wheelchair, for several months at a minimum. I spoke with our members, and we agreed that if he wants to come back, if necessary we will all chip in to install a barrier-free lift so he can use our basement location. I could have told him I would do it, but I thought it was important that he knew everyone was supporting him. We are on his side. His fight matters.

Hayato is a fighter. He is an inspiration. I'm honored that he included us in his fight.

Thursdays are usually my toughest workout of the week. I train with Hiraku Hori, a retired K-1 Kickboxing heavyweight. He was the Japan Champion and fought several of the most famous kickboxers in the history of the sport. He is a great coach and a great guy.

Our workouts usually consist of stretching and drills. I then do two three-minute rounds of shadow boxing, two three-minute rounds of mitts — using a padded target — followed by two three-minute rounds of pair drills, and finish up with three three-minute rounds of light sparring. Hiraku gauges his intensity to push me to my upper limits.

Last Thursday during sparring I walked into a counter kick to my left ribs. I went down gasping for breath. Nao, our super hospitable and friendly concierge, who videotapes our sparring sessions, looked at me with concern. Like in a movie, it seemed like all the people from all the classes stopped what they were doing to look at me as I crawled on the mat of our cage, trying to catch my breath.

I am over 60 years old. I knew that I was going to be sore. I knew that I would sport a big bruise on my side. I hear a count in my mind. 1,2, 3 ... I don't need to do this. I can call it quits until next week. 4, 5, 6 ... I think of Hayato. I think of our members. My fight means something. My fight inspires those around me. 7, 8, 9 ...

I get up. There is one minute and 23 seconds left in the round. I keep fighting. It's what I do. The world starts moving again. Nao relaxes. The other members refocus on their training.

I don't have to fight, but I want to. The pain I will feel reminds me that I'm alive, that my fight still has meaning. In some form or another, I will always be fighting.

So should you.

ACKNOWLEDGMENTS

If nothing else, this memoir provides a record of the people I am indebted to. So many people have given to me, and I hope this book shows my appreciation.

To my business partners, thank you. To Robert Roche and Tadashi Nakamura, for allowing me to lead, and to Dave Wilkey for calling me away from my oblivion on Wall Street so we could start our first business.

As a leader, I would be nothing without followers. No words can express my honor and gratitude to my Oak Lawn Marketing comrades. With Billy's Bootcamp, Core Rhythm, TRF Easy-to-Dance, True Sleeper, Hill's Diet, Bare Escentuals and other iconic hit products too numerous to mention, we changed Japan and had tremendous fun doing it.

To my business partnerships, past and current, with special mention to Avex, Hakuhodo, Flying Machine, Genius, Ever Sports, Rakuten, Genius, Thane, Body Orbit, Fitness Quest, Think Fitness, the UFC Gym, Spice Up Fitness and Leo Wealth.

To my secretarial team, thank you for making me up my game to give me 'rizz.'

To my Shorinji Kempo dojo-mates at Cornell, New York Doin, Hakusan Doin, Meito Doin and Nagakute Minami Doin for taking an 'outsider' and bringing him inside. To Heat and Bunge for training and providing opportunities for me as a fighter.

My heartfelt thanks go out to the people of Japan. This country, my home, has provided me with a livelihood, a place to raise my family and live the Japanese dream. I hope you feel that I am making a difference, and making Japan a better place.

I have had the honor to work with the US-Japan Conference on Cultural and Educational Interchange, the Japan-US Friendship Commission, US-Japan Bridging Foundation, Hope International Development Agency Japan, The American Chamber of Commerce Japan, The Japan Association of Corporate Executives, and The Electronic Retailer's Association. All these organizations have a purpose that I believe in. Shared purpose and passion have allowed me to learn and build a meaningful network within these groups.

Books have made a difference in my life. Some of the books and authors that shaped me as a businessman are *Good to Great*, *Tribal Leadership*, *Delivering Happiness*, and *The Signal and the Noise*. Books that inspired my love affair with Japan are *Shogun* and the James Clavell novels, *Japan as #1*, and more recently the John Rain novels by Barry Eisler. I also got a lot out of books that inform the human experience, including *The Lord of the Rings*, the novels of William Faulkner and Gabriel García Márquez, and the poetry of William Butler Yeats.

Many individuals or groups have supported and inspired me: Mikihiko Mizuno, Shinji Hayashi, Tak Niinami, Hayato Fujita Jr, Kazue Osada, Nameless Theatre, Torakukai, Steven Feinberg, Jonny Reed, Micha Riss, Nancy Stark, The Titans, The Never Too Late Academy, Flexwerk

Fitness, SBC Holdings, Hiroshi Mikitani, Dustin Schnabel, August Hergensheimer, Scott Reid, Konoshiki, John Sasaki, Jonathan Krakoff, Anthony Ferrante, and so many others I'm inevitably forgetting.

Most importantly, 1 am grateful to my family. My full array of parents: my mother, father and stepfather, Dick, who have passed away; my stepmother, Lyn, who still calls me an idiot; my sister, Morissa, who we lost too soon; my sister and brother, Effie and Tim, and their families; and all my aunts, uncles and cousins.

Family defines me. Love and thanks to my children, Ken, Rian, Ellie, Mari, Sean and their significant others; my grandchildren, Amy and Taiga; and Rian's dogs, Abba and Mellow. You are my pride and inspiration.

Thank you, Yumiko, for teaching me the true meaning of the word gratitude.

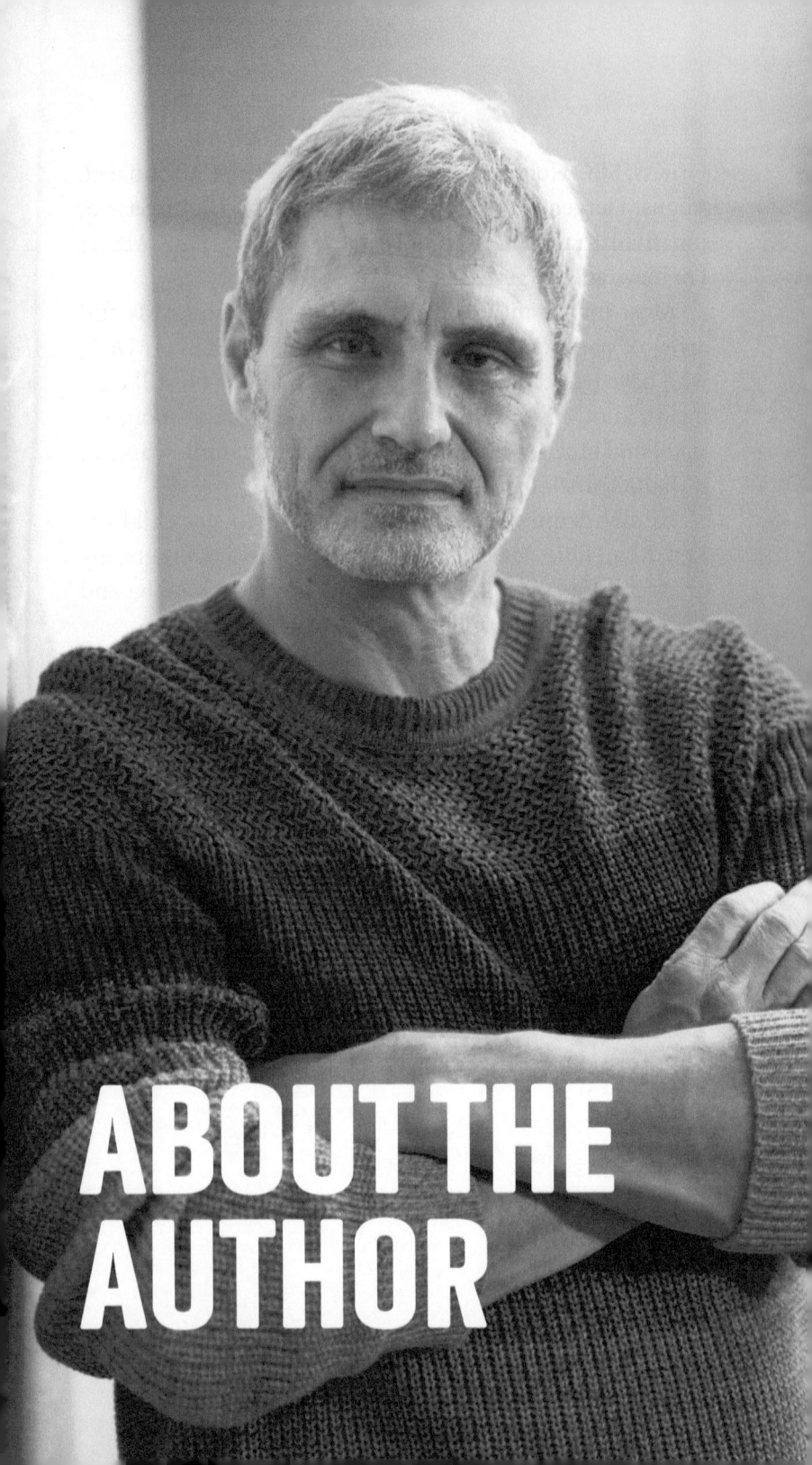

ABOUT THE AUTHOR

Harry A. Hill, a dynamic business and civic leader, is renowned as one of Japan's most successful foreign entrepreneurs. His pivotal role in the growth of Oak Lawn Marketing, Inc. is a testament to his leadership skills and business acumen. As the President and CEO from 2006 to 2017, he steered the company to a remarkable increase in sales, from ¥15 billion to ¥68 billion. His strategic prowess was further demonstrated in 2009, when he orchestrated one of the largest M&A transactions of the year, leading to NTT Docomo's acquisition of a 51% share in OLM. Hill's legacy at OLM continues, as he now serves as an outside director, contributing his insights and experience.

Hill is co-founder of Better-U, the master franchiser of the UFC Gym in Japan. Better-U's vision is that fitness and education are lifelong endeavors, and it is never too late to "version me up." The first corporate-owned UFC Gym location opened in April 2020, three days before the national state of emergency announcement because of the COVID-19 pandemic. Despite the challenges of opening during the Covid-19 pandemic, the UFC gyms have seen steady growth. There are two corporate-owned locations in the Tokyo area, and the first franchise opened in Gifu in 2023.

Hill is active both as a business and civic leader. The White House Department of Personnel appointed him as Co-Chair of The U.S.-Japan Conference on Cultural and Educational Interchange (CULCON). This binational advisory panel elevates and strengthens the vital cultural and educational foundations of the U.S.-Japan relationship and strengthens connections between U.S. and Japanese leadership in those fields. He has also served as Chairman of the Japan-U.S. Friendship Commission, Chairman of the Electronic Retailer's Association, Governor of the American Chamber of Commerce of Japan, Vice Chair of the U.S.-Japan Bridging Foundation, board member of the U.S. JET Alumni Association, and past Chair and current board member of HOPE International Development Agency, Japan.

Harry A. Hill's commitment to empowering others is a constant motif in his business and personal life. His role as a Male Champion of Change, recognized for promoting gender diversity, underscores his commitment to equality and empowerment. During his tenure as Chairman of HOPE International Development Agency, Japan, Hill was passionate about providing clean water for the neglected poor in underdeveloped countries. When disaster struck in Japan on March 11, 2011, he championed the creation of the Genki Japan fund, which helped 77 different groups and individuals rebuild their livelihoods. One of the Genki Japan fund recipients best encapsulated Hill's philosophy, "If we get help to rebuild our means to make a living, we can rebuild our homes and communities ourselves. We don't want handouts; we want to be self-reliant."

In both business and civic activities, the themes of self-reliance, empowerment, education, fitness, and an optimistic vision for the future drive Hill. In Japanese, two of his favorite words are the homonym *Souzou*(想像/創造). The first character means to imagine, and the second character means to plan and build. Hill's management and leadership philosophy couples a meaningful goal and purpose with a concrete roadmap. The two words must coexist for sustained success. He also demands adherence to the 2Ps, purpose and profit, at all times.

Hill's influence extends beyond his business and civic activities. He is a frequent speaker at to both business and academic groups and is the author of two books, with his most recent work being *Fighter! A Guide to Life and Business*. His writings offer unique insights into his life and business philosophy, making them a must-read for those interested in entrepreneurship and leadership.